Snake Dancing

Roberta Sykes

ALLEN & UNWIN

First published in 1998 by
Allen & Unwin Pty Ltd
9 Atchison Street, St Leonards, NSW 1590 Australia
Phone: (61 2) 8425 0100
Fax: (61 2) 9906 2218
E-mail: frontdesk@allen-unwin.com.au
Web: http://www.allen-unwin.com.au

National Library of Australia
Cataloguing-in-Publication entry:

Sykes, Roberta B.
    Snake dancing.

    ISBN 1 86448 837 9

    1. Sykes, Roberta B. 2. Authors, Australian—Biography.
    3. Aborigines, Australian—Civil rights. 4. Aborigines,
    Australian—Land tenure. 5. Afro-Americans—Australia—
    Biography. 6. Afro-American women—Australia—Biography.
    I. Title. (Series: Sykes, Roberta B. Snake dreaming; v. 2).

920.009296073

Set in 12/15 pt Novarese
Printed by Australian Print Group

10 9 8 7 6 5 4 3

There's a devil in me who shouts,
and I do what he says,
whenever I feel I'm choking with some emotion
He says: 'DANCE!'
And I dance. And I feel better!
Once, when my little Dimitraki died in Chalcidice,
I got up as I did a moment ago and I danced.
The relations and friends who saw me
Dancing in front of the body
Rushed up to stop me.
'ZORBA HAS GONE MAD!'
But if at that moment I had not danced,
I should really have gone mad—from grief.

Zorba the Greek
Nikos Kazantzakis

1

The Sunlander rattled its way south overnight to Brisbane. I sat, eyes glued to the window, watching the darkened North Queensland landscape speed by. How many times now had I made this long train trip from Townsville? Two nights and one day—a lot of time in which to reflect on the past and try to summon up the energy for the exciting future which I was sure lay ahead.

My second marriage seemed irrevocably beyond repair and I was formulating my next moves on the run. I was en route to Sydney, hopefully to become a journalist. I had sent a small number of articles I'd written down to publishers in Sydney, including *Pol* and *Readers Digest*, but had not heard back from any of them. I also planned to join up with the fledgling Black movement. First a brief stopover in Brisbane to meet with the charismatic Denis Walker, who had made a political visit to Townsville a few weeks earlier, and then on to only the heavens knew what.

I should have been sleeping. My two-year-old daughter, Naomi, was sprawled in the adjoining seat, her head cradled on my lap. Keeping her occupied on this cramped train throughout the next day would severely tax me. Yet my mind was too full of imagery, memories and anguish to relax and try to sleep.

Mum's voice penetrated my thoughts: 'Nobody has a right to ask you your business—unless you are asking them for something.' She had told me this many times. 'If you want to borrow money from a bank, they'll ask you your business. Same if you want a loan from anyone or want to get the dole.'

Her advice was reassuring—I had a lot of 'business' I wished to keep secret. Brutally beaten to within an inch of my life, gang-raped and left for dead, discarded in a shack in the bush, I had risen up from the blood-ied soil to put four of the perpetrators behind bars. As a result of the attack I had given birth to a son, Russel, who had become the centre of my world and the reason for my existence. Only by mentally distancing him and myself from the event, I reasoned, would he be able to grow up unencumbered by any knowledge of the actrocity by which he had joined me. He was now safely at boarding school in Charters Towers, while I was heading south with his sister to try to set up a new life for us all. I did not want the past to rise up and ruin whatever chances were ahead for us, hence my own 'secret business'.

Earlier on, Mum's advice had only proved partially correct. When I had first appeared around the town with my child, people's heads had turned. 'Is this *your* baby? I didn't know you were married!' Many people in Townsville, some of whom I had known since I was a small girl, regarded themselves somehow as my friends, as country people do, and felt familiar enough to ask their questions.

Friendly inquiries perhaps, but to me they had registered as gross intrusions into my privacy, and I often had to manufacture an acceptable answer to draw the conversation away from their nosiness.

Mum's advice, over the years, had been a mixture of both the wise and the injudicious. Only with hindsight was I able to distinguish which category had been given to me on each occasion.

After the birth of my son, Mum had taken it upon herself to find me 'a suitable husband'. When I'd rejected her choice of spouse, George Dean, a soccer-playing Englishman, she had nagged and intimidated me.

'Roberta, you're eighteen years old and with a child in tow. Not a very attractive proposition for a wife, my girl, and you're getting older every day. If you don't fix your mind right, you're going to be left on the shelf. You'll be an old maid and your life will be miserable, I tell you now. Stop this snooty manner you go on with and at least be polite when men talk to you!'

During these harangues, Mum chose to overlook the fact that, little more than a year earlier, I'd been so severely traumatised by my experiences that the police were recommending I be committed to a psychiatric hospital. Now she told me to embrace life and become the smiling, happy young woman she so desperately wanted me to be. Perhaps she felt she could *force* me to become that person.

Skip, whom I'd met just days before the birth of my son, often came by the house to pay court. Mum began inviting him to meals, and he started to escort me to movies on weekends, carrying Russel in one arm and the bag of baby essentials on the other. He was quite taken by the fact that men and women always stood up for him when we rode into town on the bus, to enable him to sit comfortably with the infant.

Alone, he was in no way threatening, always gentle and almost shy in manner. He was also strikingly good-looking, like one of those baby-faced Hollywood stars who played in the films we went to see.

Mum swooped on the attention he was paying me and the baby as an indication of his good intentions. 'He'd make a fine husband,' she told me, 'and he's a very popular soccer player.' He played in, and helped coach, one of the local teams. On weekends Mum plotted to get me to the soccer field to watch him play, often arranging to have Arthur, her boyfriend, pick me up from town where I'd been shopping. Only then would she tell me that they were on their way to watch a game and would not be able to take me back to the house until it was over. I'd learned that Skip played centre forward, but apart from that I knew little about soccer and was totally disinterested in any sports which involved grown men chasing around a field after a ball. Still Mum persisted.

When Skip began to put his arm around me at the pictures and embrace me when he was leaving the house, I grew cold. I told Mum I couldn't stand to be touched.

'It's not hard,' she said. 'Just think about something else. You don't have to lead a man. They know what to do.'

'Think of what?' I couldn't tell her that every time I closed my eyes I was back in a darkened shack, that fear rose up in my throat and almost choked me.

'Think about what shopping you need. Compile a shopping list in your head,' Mum advised.

This became a sort of password that she whispered

to me as Skip carried the sleeping baby out the door on our way to the pictures. 'And don't forget to make out that shopping list,' she'd say. On our return, Mum would make a pot of tea for us and then drag Arthur off to bed, so Skip and I could sit on the back stairs in privacy. 'Oh, and you won't forget that shopping list I wanted, will you?' would be her parting remark.

Compiling a shopping list was more difficult for me than Mum could ever have imagined. Much like a visit to the dentist, I would sit quiet and frozen, concentrating on willing myself to disappear, preparing my mind to project itself elsewhere.

Eventually, after much effort and secret anguish, not to mention Skip's extraordinary patience, I was able to compile a shopping list. Willing one's self into a state beyond consciousness and caution is one way to become pregnant, and when I did, Mum was elated. I was thrown back into the cave with the demons.

On hearing the news Skip took off, back to his family in Newcastle. However, he wrote daily and said he would send for me as soon as he could sort himself out, find a job, tell his family and get their approval. Then, he said, we would get married. Mum said this wouldn't do, and she gave me the bus fare so Russel and I could go to Newcastle. I was apprehensive as I'd never been further south than Brisbane and knew no one across the border.

As Skip and I were both under twenty-one we could not marry without parental consent, so Mum wrote me a letter of consent. She said it was unlikely that Skip could afford a wedding ring, so she took a plain gold band out of the handbag in which she kept her treasures and gave it to me. 'Wear it on the bus down,' she told me. 'It will help keep the stickybeaks from wanting to know your business.'

We had to travel almost two thousand miles. It was a long trip, broken only by a few hours stopover with Mum's sister, Aunty Glad, in Brisbane. Her house in South Brisbane was just a few blocks from the bus depot, I was able to take a shower and re-stock Russel's food and travel bag. He was a delightful baby, sitting up and taking an interest in everything we passed on the journey, and sleeping soundly for hours, which enabled me also to get some rest.

The bus had been scheduled to arrive at Broadmeadows at around 3 am. I had no idea how far Broadmeadows was from Newcastle, nor how I would get from there to Wallsend, where Skip was living. In my letter telling him I was coming, I'd said I'd phone him when I arrived. Now, having seen some of the deserted spots at which passengers were being picked up and put down, I began to worry whether there would even be a phone, and about the embarrassment of ringing the number he had given me, at his aunt's house, at such an ungodly hour.

On a stretch of road about two hours away from Broadmeadows, one of the passengers suddenly shouted for the bus to stop; he had heard a cry for help coming from the roadside. The driver pulled up short, passengers were roused from their sleep, and some men on board walked back along the road to see what had happened. To everyone's surprise and dismay, a car had run off the road and crashed into a tree, trapping the occupants inside. The unfortunate travellers in the car could have waited there in the dark until morning or death, whichever came first. One of the occupants, on regaining consciousness, had screamed out as we went by and, almost miraculously, the passenger on our bus had heard him.

We all gave over our travel blankets to cover the injured people and keep them warm, and the next car along the road was flagged down and sent to the nearest police station and to raise the ambulance. The car's driver, a young man, and his female companion were trapped by their legs under the dashboard. A second couple, in the back, were concussed and battered but able to be pulled to safety.

Because of the delay, the bus arrived at Broadmeadow just on dawn, which was a great relief to me. The Broadmeadows stop was marked only by a pole beside the road—no shelter, no phone. Had we arrived as scheduled I would have been too terrified to get off the bus. The driver told me to walk down the highway to a corner and wait there because eventually a taxi would come by. I did so, carrying my suitcase in one hand, and my baby and his travel gear in the other. I strapped our now badly stained travel rug to the outside of the case.

The taxi dropped us at the address Skip had given me just as the family was rising, but Skip wasn't there. I learned that his aunt, uncle and nephews lived at this house, but Skip was staying a short distance away with his grandmother. If his aunt and uncle were stunned by the arrival of a thin young black girl with a baby in her arms asking for their nephew, they certainly didn't show it. Indeed, I was very surprised at their apparently relaxed attitude and the trouble they took to accommodate me and the needs of my child. Skip's uncle set out by car to fetch him while his aunt helped me bathe and feed Russel and put him down to sleep.

If the family held any discussions to decide what to

do with me, I was not included in them. I showered and dressed nicely, and Skip took me into Wallsend to show me places he had told me about, such as the local milkbar which had a jukebox with all his favourite songs. He introduced me to a few of his friends whom we met on the street.

In the afternoon his aunt told me that I was to stay with Skip's grandmother, and that Skip was moving back to her house to leave his grandmother's spare room vacant for me. Carrying Russel, I was driven to his grandmother's house where I met a charming lady over eighty years old. She welcomed us warmly and made tea. I was soon sleeping soundly in the comfortable old double bed in her second bedroom.

Skip's father was a Mason and, so Skip soon told me, a racist. He refused to meet me and refused to give his permission for us to marry. Furthermore, he said that if Skip went ahead and got court permission to marry me, he would disinherit him.

As soon as I had recovered from my travel exhaustion, I began to be troubled by insomnia. Each night, after the old lady went to bed and the house was in darkness, I lay in bed and cried. When at last I'd fall into a fitful sleep for a short time, the demons of my earlier nightmares would appear in my dreams and I'd wake again, terrified and sweating. Demons' laughter rang in my ears and I was unable to rest or go back to sleep. A makeshift crib had been put on the floor beside the bed. Russel, though not yet able to walk, could climb over any barrier and may have fallen onto the floor if he had slept on a bed. I spent nights looking down at him, watching his small chest rising and falling, his dark eyelashes curled on his cheeks.

During the daytime, too, I had 'shocks'. Sitting talking or even walking down the street, a flash would go through my mind, like a bright light. When it was over I could only recall a feeling of shock and a memory of the light, though I was told that a look of horror would come over my face and would last several seconds. This was a great surprise to me because I had the impression that this tremor was only going through my mind. After a few of these episodes, I was left feeling that there was some other memory lingering there, something just out of my grasp.

I was unable to look for a job, and Skip had not found work either. When I had been in Newcastle a little over a week, the family decided that I should go to a government office and ask for a relief cheque so that Skip's grandmother would not have the added burden of feeding Russel and me, and so that I'd have a little cash in my purse.

Although I appreciated their concern and I felt very obliged to try to please them in return, I was overwhelmed with reluctance at their suggestion. I didn't want to have to explain my business to anyone, particularly not to some strange white person who didn't know anything about me.

Notwithstanding my efforts to delay taking this step, and torn between fear and my desire to please, I was accompanied by Skip's aunt to the social security office where arrangements were made for me to be interviewed by a departmental officer. Skip's aunt then left me to return to her own house duties. The despondency that descended upon my soul as I sat in that sterile room was even darker than the gloomy room itself.

At last the officer ushered me into another dark

room where he sat behind his desk and began to ply me with questions, writing my answers on the pages in front of him. Russel lay asleep on my lap. After I told him my name and the old lady's address, the man began to show his disapproval when I told him my age and that the baby was mine. He asked me how I had been supporting myself. I explained that I'd been down from Townsville only a week and that I had received payment for being a witness in some recent court cases, but that money had now run out. Dread flooded through me when he insisted that I tell him more of my business. When I declined, it was obvious that he chose to disbelieve me. He asked about my plans, to which I replied that Skip and I were intending to marry but that Skip needed to find work before we could do so.

I felt very battered as I left the office, even though I now had a food coupon in my hand. The officer's parting remarks and stern warning were probably departmental policy, but I was wounded by them anyway. 'You can use the coupons only to purchase groceries at a store nearest to where you live—and you aren't allowed to get cigarettes. And don't come back—you can only have that one voucher.' If he had asked me, he would have found out that I was not a smoker. Instead, the way he threw these comments after me as I walked from the room left me feeling like dirt and with no way to reply.

I found my way back to the old lady's house and lay down on the bed to recover from the ordeal of the interview. This was not, I thought, how I wanted to live. Without dignity and under pressure to retell my story to strangers in order to get money to feed this child; I was extremely dispirited. I knew that even if I had told this man the details, he would have taken it upon himself to be the judge and jury. Without the weight of evidence supplied by all the other witnesses, as had occurred in the Supreme Court, I, not my assailants, may have been found guilty by this departmental officer. But guilty of what? Of having had a child out of wedlock? Or of making up stories to cover my indiscretions?

When I showed the old lady the food coupon, she said she'd arrange for Skip's uncle to pick me up at the supermarket in the morning to save me carrying home both the baby and the food. We had dinner, played with Russel for a short while, and as soon as he looked ready to sleep, we all went to bed.

Again I lay in the darkness, my mind fretfully covering all the old ground and looking for pathways ahead. The 'shocks' had been coming on me more regularly now. When I wasn't wondering if I was, in fact, going crazy, I panicked that my subconscious was harbouring traumatic memories from the night of the attack which lay deep below the surface. I could not see them, but they were erupting inside me. I was tired, very tired, and my problems seemed awesome.

The grandmother's house was brick and built close to the ground. I heard a noise at the window and lay terrified in the dark. The window slipped up and Skip climbed in. He was familiar with how to get into and out of this room without disturbing the old lady.

Finger to his lips, he nimbly stepped around Russel's makeshift crib on the floor and made his way to the bed where he lay down beside me. In a whisper he told me that he had spoken again with his father, and that his father remained adamant Skip would not marry 'a dark girl' with his consent. His father was now offering me money to go away.

Tears flowed down my face as Skip quietly talked,

telling me that he loved me but he now thought it better if I took up his father's offer. I could not speak and just lay there in silence. I remembered stories he had told me in Townsville about how his father had, through his connections, paid police not to proceed with a prosecution against Skip when he'd been caught in some youthful mischief a year or so earlier. But it shocked me that he would try to buy me off, thereby making a bastard of his own grandchild and leaving the child to its own fate.

When he had finished telling what his father had said, Skip left through the window as silently as he had arrived. After he had gone, I had no thoughts, only feelings. The weight of my world was upon me. One unasked for child lay sleeping on the floor beside me; one I was unable even to feed without subjecting myself to the interrogation of hostile strangers. Now, another child, equally unloved by its father and his family, was beginning to grow in my womb. If I relaxed one iota, I feared a 'shock' would come upon me, and whatever new memories arose might push me beyond help. Not one fragment of hope was found anywhere on my horizon.

For as long as I could I lay there supporting this weight, then I realised it was too heavy, even for me. I climbed off the bed and scrambled through my suitcase until I found the strong leather strap with which I'd secured the bloodied travel blanket to its side. On the back of the door was an old-fashioned sturdy metal coat hook, and I fashioned a loop and slid the strap around the hook. Standing on a small stool I pulled the loop tightly around my neck and stepped off, hopefully into oblivion.

For just a moment I hung there, suspended in the

wave of spinning dizziness. I had become familiar with this sensation during my choking episodes throughout my pregnancy. Then I was suddenly and effortlessly speeding towards a very bright light. A feeling of joy flooded into me as I whisked through the air. As I came nearer the light, I saw silhouettes, in fact quite a crowd of people were waiting there. I knew they were waiting for me and that I was smiling. Radiance and warmth flooded through me. I could hear a sound that was not music but which was extremely pleasant. I was getting closer and closer to the crowd, which was growing nearer in my vision, but not clear enough for me to recognise anyone.

Inexplicably I was suddenly spinning and dropping away fast. It took only a fraction of a second before I heard a muffled thump. I was confused, bewildered. The wonderful joy I had experienced was somehow pouring out of me and the brilliant light had disappeared. I opened my eyes to see it again, to get my bearings, to resume my journey towards it, but instead I saw just a ray of electric light coming from a partly opened door in front of me. It was being pushed and shoved against my feet.

A deep voice spoke quietly from the other side of the door, and in that second I realised I was back on earth and that I had failed in my attempt to end my misery.

Skip's uncle, a pastor in the Re-organised Church of Latter Day Saints, said he had been resting at home when he had been overcome with a feeling of great urgency that he had to go immediately to the old lady's house. As he ran up the path towards the unlit house he had seen a light go on and had tapped on the front door. He and the old lady had heard a thud and had pushed my bedroom door open to investigate.

I was laying on the floor, blood seeping through my night clothes at the elbows and knees where they had flailed against the door panels when I entered the throes. The strap was still fastened tightly around my neck and the other end was around the hook, which had been wrenched from the door with the exertion of the thrashing of my strangulation.

Sheltering her from seeing me on the floor, Skip's uncle sent the old lady away to make us all a cup of tea. Then, without so much as one word of reproach, he removed the strap and helped me up onto my shaking legs.

The uncle sat with me in the lounge room in silence, his head bowed. When she came in old lady's eyes were red from crying. We sipped the sweet milky tea and sat quietly. Later the old lady brought a dampened washer for me to wipe my face and sponge the blood off my clothes. After an indeterminable length of time, the uncle said simply, 'Let us pray.' I was not familiar with the words of his prayer, which seemed to go for a while. Then he again helped me to my feet and directed me towards the bedroom. At the doorway he put his arm around my shoulder and said words I had been longing to hear for years, 'Go to sleep now. Everything will be alright.'

Strangely, the noise of my body thrashing wildly against the door had failed to wake Russel, though the old lady, whose hearing was not so wonderful, had been awakened by it through two walls. Seeing Russel sleeping so quietly and peacefully flooded me with guilt. Only then was I able to shed my tears and fall asleep.

Next morning, as promised, I took the government food voucher and a list to the supermarket to replenish supplies which we had eaten in the old lady's house and to buy other essentials. Skip's uncle picked us up and drove us home. I was shocked to learn from the old lady that the police had been to the house asking for me during my absence. They hadn't told her what they wanted and were coming back later in the afternoon.

I was surprised, on opening the door to their knock, to find two large policemen in dark uniforms with big guns strapped to their hips. In Queensland at that time police did not usually wear guns and I was intimidated at the sight of them. I had to attend yet another court hearing in Brisbane related to the rapists' trials. Mum had redirected the orders and travel warrants to the Newcastle police station, and these officers had come to deliver them. I was to leave the next day. The police thumped their boots awkwardly down the flower-bordered path on the way back to their car.

When I told the old lady how shocked I was about New South Wales police wearing guns, she said that her neighbour had called the police when some children stole her child's tricycle. When they turned up wearing guns to deal with such a minor incident involving kids, she had withdrawn her complaint and asked them to leave. I was relieved to hear I wasn't the only person who had this reaction.

On my return from Brisbane a few days later Skip told me that he had arranged a court hearing to get permission to marry. We went together and he explained our circumstances and was given court permission. His uncle offered to perform the ceremony, and preparations were set in train. I wrote to tell Mum and she sent me a frock belonging to my sister, Dellie, that she felt was suitable to be married in as I had no money to buy anything new. For a gift she sent the bus fare for Skip, Russel and me to return to Townsville.

She felt that as Skip had not found work in Newcastle, he would have a better chance of getting a job in the north where work for men was plentiful.

While waiting for the hasty wedding arrangements to be completed Skip's grandmother took it upon herself to keep me company. She apologised profusely when, for one day, she had to leave me alone in order to visit her mother. I must admit when I first heard this I thought it may have been a ruse as this old lady herself was over eighty, but no, her mother was the oldest person in Newcastle, over one hundred years of age. I was fascinated with the idea that someone could have lived so long and, on the old lady's return, I asked how they had spent the day. 'Oh,' she replied, 'we had a cup of tea and a chat. Then we had a little lie down. We made lunch together and then had another little lie down. We had another cup of tea before I caught the bus home.' The thought of these two old women sipping tea and having a lie down together, mother and daughter, at their great age conjured up for me a serenity and a peace with the world which I realised I would probably never know.

On another day the old lady insisted we go to the pictures. I was surprised again when the film she was so keen to see turned out to be *The Hustler*. 'Oh, I just *love* Paul Newman. I see him in everything,' she told me on the bus on the way in. Watching a quite violent film about poolroom hustling and revenge was not how I thought old ladies filled their days.

Our wedding was a modest affair. It was organised by Skip's family who appeared warm and friendly, and some of his relatives whom I had not met before attended. No one had made even the slightest reference to my attempt to kill myself. I think they knew in their hearts and minds that my actions were not manipulative—I had just reached the point of being unable to bear any more pain in my life.

Skip's aunt told me before the ceremony that, following the wedding, I was to return with Skip to her house. However, Skip would continue to share the room with her two adolescent sons and Russel and I were to stay in the little sleep-out at the back of the house. The aunt explained that she did not want her boys becoming curious and asking questions about sex before she was ready to answer them.

So, apart from moving my suitcase from one house to another, there was no real difference in my life following my marriage. In the few days before we left for Queensland Skip's aunt gave me many useful cooking hints. This was one area of my education that Mum had badly overlooked, favouring my youngest sister, Leonie, in the kitchen. When Skip's aunt found out I had no idea even how to boil vegetables, she taught me that the density of a vegetable determined how long it would take to cook, and that to determine the density all I had to do was to squeeze each one gently, then place them in a pot of boiling water in order, for example, hard carrots first, with soft green vegetables last. I was really pleased to learn some basic culinary skills because Russel was becoming dissatisfied with bottled baby foods, preferring to munch on almost anything off my plate.

The bus trip home exhausted me, although Skip relieved me of the responsibility of holding my increasingly inquisitive and active child on my knee throughout the journey. When I'd arrived in Newcastle Russel had been crawling and hauling himself onto his feet, but during my brief stay at Skip's aunt's house he had one day launched himself across the room from his standing position and had taken more than half a dozen steps before abruptly falling down on his bottom. He had looked around in amazement at his own triumph and found that we'd all stopped what we were doing to watch him. Then, instead of crying with the fall, he had laughed his merry chuckle of delight and accomplishment. Of course, he wanted to walk all the time, and flailed his little arms and legs to get down from the lap of whoever might be holding him so that he could have another go at toddling. It was a feat to hold him still and keep him occupied throughout the trip.

On our arrival in Townsville we initially stayed at Mum's house. Soon Skip got a job as a paymaster with Hornibrooks, a big company with a contract to build bridges under the railway line between Townsville and Mount Isa. He had to travel up and down the line, stopping at every camp and detailing the hours each man had worked and the wages he had earned. Skip badly needed major dental work and dentures, so I also hunted down a job waitressing at the Laguna Cafe.

For a few weeks this worked well, with Mum coming home from her job as laundress at the Central Hotel mid-afternoon and taking over Russel's care while I hopped on her bicycle and cycled into town to work until the cafe closed at around midnight. I had no experience in waitressing but few women were interested in working such late hours. Mum, who had worked in dining rooms sometime in her life before she had me, gave me a crash course at home. As it turned out, learning to operate a cappuccino machine would later become a distinct advantage. The routine of working in the evenings suited me too, because I was plagued with morning sickness early in the day, and I was able to be with Russel during his waking hours.

Most of the late-night customers were Mediterranean men who drank short black coffees, and some of them were very fresh. I was often afraid as I cycled home through the deserted streets all the way to Aitkenvale, but anything was better than having no income and being forced again to go through the shame of explaining myself to some government official.

Mum had divided the house she owned in Norris Street, Hermit Park, into two flats, and she encouraged us to move into one of them. With Skip settled into his job, and now living too far from Mum for her to babysit Russel, I gave up work and began to look forward to becoming a full-time housewife and mother.

My hopes were very short lived. Still suffering from trauma, I often burst into tears about trifling things, even when I was alone. I continued to have 'shocks', some of which left me unable to properly communicate with people for hours. Sometimes Mum came by after work and, seeing me so stressed, she would take Russel over to her house for the night. Early in the morning on her way to her six o'clock start, she'd bring him back and rebuke me. Russel, she told me, would wake up at her house screaming in the night from nightmares at precisely the same time as I screamed myself awake several miles distant. I was to 'settle down'.

Skip was away with his job for ten days or more at a time, and when he came home I became uptight and distressed, apprehensive about his expectations. Often, too, he would have gambled away a lot of his wages before he even reached our house. Eventually Mum told me to move back in with her until the baby was born and then to try again. Although there was a great deal of tension between me and her boyfriend, Arthur, who lived with her, I complied.

Arthur was in and out of trouble with the police. A hairdresser, his barber shop was located in a Flinders Street billiards saloon. Crooks often offered their stolen goods to him, invitations he found hard to refuse. After one such transaction the manager of an electrical goods store just a few doors down the street from the barber shop came in for a haircut and, to his astonishment, found that radios and other small electrical appliances which had been stolen from his store overnight were now on display for sale at Arthur's.

The police came to Mum's house and went through the whole place, searching for anything stolen. My youngest sister, Leonie, was extremely upset because the police, while searching her room, had shaken out her packet of Modess. She was fourteen years old and had only just arrived at the stage of needing to use them. She cried for hours with embarrassment after the police had gone.

Mum resented anything that drew the attention of the police to our family in a negative manner, and Arthur's drinking and bent habits often upset her. She packed his bags and locked him out of the house several times, but he always wormed his way back. He would sleep in the car she had bought for him, parked just around the corner, and we would see him, unshaven and unkempt for days. Then suddenly he'd be living in the house again. Mum said she needed him back to drive her to the Central Hotel in the mornings as she was getting too old to ride her bike so many miles before starting a full work day.

I was in bed in a verandah room at Mum's house one night when I felt a rush of warmth between my thighs.

For a moment I thought I had wet the bed, but when I looked I could see it was blood. I was seven months pregnant and thought the baby must be arriving early. Mum had Arthur drive me immediately to the hospital. Pains wracked my body for hours and I screamed, much to the annoyance of the other patients. But when I cried out for relief a nurse told me they were unable to give me anything because it would have been construed as 'assisting an abortion'.

All night and throughout the next day the pains continued. Suddenly a warm mass passed from me, and I called the nurse urgently. She came behind the screen which had been shielding me from the view of the other patients, and quickly bundled up the sheets and took them away. She came back to tell me, 'That was your baby', before rolling me from side to side to fit the bed out with fresh linen. When she had finished her work, she said a doctor would be coming to see me and to pronounce the baby dead. I tugged at the screen and saw an Asian doctor walk into the pan room. He then passed by on his way back towards the elevator. I called after him, 'What was the baby?' He didn't stop walking but replied, 'I didn't bother to look.' I picked up a small vase that was standing on top of my locker and hurled it towards him. It missed him and shattered on the wall. The nurse was just feet away from him and she ran back into the pan room. She came out and called from the other side of the ward, 'It was a boy.'

Over the next twenty-four hours I slept in fits and starts, an exhausted rest, in between which various nurses came by to share fragments of information with me. Although I'd been seven months pregnant, even by their own records kept in the maternity clinic of the hospital, they had marked that the child had been only thirty weeks developed. This had been done, I was told, because from thirty-two weeks I would have been put to the expense of a funeral. I was devastated that such an action could have been taken without any discussion with me. I was in mourning for my lost infant and a funeral would have given me an opportunity to express my grief and my love for this prematurely born son. The next day I got up and signed myself out of the hospital, tight-lipped, refusing to back down on my decision to leave despite their sternest warnings.

Two days later I was back in hospital, having passed out in the street, and was given a dilation and curettage.

Mum had sent for Skip when the miscarriage was imminent, and he had returned by the earliest train. What thoughts were going through his head I have no idea, because although he came to see me in the hospital he was coldly formal towards me. When I'd signed myself out of hospital we had shared a bed for just one night before he had to go back to his job, and he had rebuked me. 'That was *my* baby you just lost,' he said and turned away to sleep with his face to the wall, as though the miscarriage was something I had planned.

When I came out of hospital after the D & C, Mum could see how distressed I was and she reproached Skip about his attitude. I had the overwhelming feeling that I had to get away, to go anywhere, to disentangle myself from all the choking emotions that I seemed unable either to bear or to share. I told Mum I was going.

'I'll go to Aunty Glad's,' I said, 'and then work it out from there.' Mum agreed, but argued that I should leave Russel with her until I had straightened myself out, found a job and had somewhere of my own for him to live. Too exhausted to think, I acquiesced.

As I sat once more on the Sunlander, I recalled that earlier trip on my way to Newcastle. Travelling alone, I slept lightly almost all the way, the discomfort of the seats and the proximity of the other passengers keeping deep sleep—and the demons—at bay.

2

On the train travelling south I knew that my marriage was over. How could it have been otherwise? A traumatised Black girl of eighteen married to an equally young and inexperienced white youth, both held down with their own problems, neither in a position to assist the other. Throughout our courtship and our marriage, we had spent less than thirty days in each other's company.

I had never overcome my abhorrence of the physical side of our marriage. To put this into context, though, many women 'fake it' some of the time, and some all of the time. My spectrum of responses didn't extend to faking and instead I continued to use Mum's suggestion, compiling grocery lists. But when I lost my concentration on the list, I experienced severe flashbacks and I would scream. Skip had tried to help me by holding his hand over my mouth while he continued with his activities, telling me that when I became used to body contact things would change for me and I'd begin to like it. I couldn't see how I'd ever get past the barrier of my traumatised response, but his theory sounded reasonable and I tried to comply.

Still, many pleasant and even humorous events stood out in my memories of our time together. I recalled walking on the Esplanade in Townsville one warm evening with Skip, my sister, Dellie, and a young man she was dating. We'd come downtown to look at a new fountain that had just been installed. Afterwards, we ran beneath the trees, with Dellie and her boyfriend, both tall, jumping high to try to touch the overhanging leaves. A police car pulled up, but we were laughing amongst ourselves and barely noticed it. Two officers got out and approached us. They separated us, one policeman questioning Dellie and me, while the other took the lads a fair distance away and spoke to them. Suddenly we saw the officer leave Skip and Dellie's boyfriend and walk hastily back towards the car, calling to his colleague to join him.

The guys, bent over with laughter, returned. The policeman, Skip informed us, had, after asking them for their names, warned them sternly about 'hanging around with the darkies', chiding them that they would end up with no good. Skip said he listened intently and politely to the lecture, at the end of which he told the officer that his advice was too late. 'What do you mean, too late?' 'Well, it's too late, mate. I've already married her,' he replied, and the red-faced policeman had been forced to take his leave. We laughed about this for weeks.

On another fine day Skip and I had taken a ferry to Magnetic Island, one of my favourite destinations, where we walked to an almost deserted beach. We clambered over rocks until we found the right one, large and smooth, and we spread our towels and laid there soaking up the sun. When it became too hot, we walked and splashed in the clear blue water, then we sauntered off to the nearest kiosk to fill up with sandwiches and cold drinks. The day had been so magic, so full of peace, that I'd cried from relief on the return ferry late in the afternoon. I had not had one 'shock' or flashback the whole day.

There had also been some bad times, such as the Christmas Eve when Skip turned up at the house having gambled away every last penny of his pay. I had been expecting to be able to buy presents and enough food to last throughout the festive season. We had made arrangements to have Christmas lunch with Dessie and Reg Mills and their children, with Dessie providing the food and Skip and I supplying the drinks. I had been too distraught and embarrassed even to ring them to say we couldn't go. When Mum came by in the late afternoon on her way home from work I had begged her to take Russel to her house for Christmas as we had nothing to eat at our place. Dessie saved us from an absolutely miserable Christmas Day by coming for us anyway, refusing to take no for an answer.

Initially I had been very pleased to be married. I hadn't welcomed the physical aspect, indeed dreaded the prospect, but I liked being called 'Mrs' and the superficial legitimacy I felt this cast over my son. I had told Skip about the rape, though not the horror details which I had not been able to think about, much less talk about. Also, I had to explain to him why Mum and I had to travel to Brisbane for the court hearings. On several occasions, I pressed him to agree that he would never turn Russel away, no matter what happened to us, to our marriage; that he would allow Russel to think that Skip was his father. However, even as he made the promise, my heart told me that I could place no weight on his agreement.

Our relationship had been doomed from the start. I had not been aware of the depth of my mental anguish, and no one with whom I came into contact had any idea that professional counselling may have been required to help me find my way out of the maze.

After I had left Skip and was staying at Aunty Glad's, I realised that I needed a job, and I decided to follow my earlier career path and try to get back into nursing. I went to the Mater Hospital, only a short distance from Aunty Glad's house, and was given four weeks work relieving a maternity clinic nurse while she was on holidays. The job gave me a month's grace. Each morning I put on my uniform and my nurse's serene face and went to the hospital. There I greeted pregnant women who came in for their regular clinic visits, tested their urine, recorded their temperature and blood pressure and helped them prepare for their examination by the clinic doctor.

I wrote to my childhood friend Leila Laaksonen, who was working in Sydney at a private hospital at Turra-murra, and asked her about the possibility of finding work as a nurse in New South Wales. She replied enthusiastically and encouraged me to come down as soon as my stint at the Mater Hospital was completed. I began to feel more secure; I had plans.

On the last day of my four weeks at the hospital, the clinic sister posted the shift roster for the following week and my name was still on it. When I asked her about it, she said, 'Oh, the patients love you and you're a good worker. We'd be delighted to keep you. Hasn't anybody said anything to you about this yet?'

I was very reluctant to leave. The job was pleasant,

my workmates were friendly, and I enjoyed seeing the women and feeling that I was assisting them all, new mothers-to-be and old timers, each with their different stories and attitudes. But I had written Leila that I'd be there within the week, she had replied with the offer of a place to stay in the flat she shared with other nurses at Coogee, and I felt committed to these plans. The opportunity to stay on at the Mater Hospital had come just a few days too late.

By the time I'd paid Aunty Glad for my board and sent a few pounds to Mum to cover Russel's needs, my store of cash looked slim and I was concerned that I wouldn't have enough to tide me over in Sydney until I had found another job. Leila, I knew, was a poor money manager, and it would have been folly to rely on her for food as well as a bed. With this in mind, I decided to hitch a lift to Sydney to save cash, and went out with my suitcase to the highway on the edge of Brisbane where Aunty Glad had told me there was a truckies' stop.

I spoke to one of the women working at the truckies' cafe about getting a lift to Sydney. She pointed out a driver who she said was a decent guy and would give me no trouble. The man was as good as his word, and by mid-morning next day we had arrived at the outskirts of Sydney. However, tired from the long haul he had missed the weigh-in station, a fact to which he was alerted by the sharp sound of a siren behind him. Pulling off to the side of the road, he quickly slid my case across the floor of the cabin and, without even time to say thanks, I jumped out and tripped off down the road to nearby Hornsby station.

One of Leila's two flatmates arrived home to find me sitting on the stairs and she let me in. I could tell she was surprised to see me. Leila had told them that her 'sister' was coming to stay a while so they were expecting a white girl. When Leila came home that evening she immediately asked me for money towards the rent. I didn't have a room, but I could sleep in an alcove between the lounge and kitchen. It held a narrow seat which doubled for a bed for someone as thin as I was, with a little space beside it in which to stow my suitcase. I'd soon find a job, she said, and then get my own place.

The three women flatting together were all nurses and worked different shifts in different hospitals around the city. Most of the time there was no one at home. I checked out some of the private hospitals which Leila had suggested but found they were more interested in having me mop their floors than attend to their patients. It wasn't hard to see they weren't prepared to employ a Black in a nursing capacity.

My experience so far had been in public hospitals, and they were usually more centrally located than the private ones, so I put my name down at Sydney Hospital in Macquarie Street in the city. Leila was blatantly envious when a letter arrived just a few days later asking me to come in for an interview. Still, despite her often odd behaviour in Townsville when we were children, I did not suspect anything.

However, on the day of the interview, I found my references from Charters Towers and Brisbane Mater hospitals missing from my suitcase. I was alarmed—they were my passport to work! I had taken them with me to the private hospitals, now they had disappeared. No one else was at home, so I phoned Leila at work. She told me I was stupid, of course no one had taken them, and it was my own fault if I was unable to find them.

ROBERTA SYKES

Red-eyed, I went in to the interview anyway. The sister was pleased with the wide range of my experience, gained mostly at Charters Towers, and my obvious familiarity with nursing and maternity terminology. But without my papers she was unable to employ me. She came up with another suggestion: would I consider working as a waitress in the nurses' dining room until I wrote away and got copies of my nursing references?

The idea was unappealing but I agreed. I thought about how difficult it would be later to establish my status as a nurse amongst women who had grown used to me serving up their meals and taking away their dirty plates. However, I had very little money left, having given the bulk of my meagre savings to Leila for rent in advance. Most of all, I did not want to have to humble myself by going to a government agency. A job was a job, and the offer of a better position in the future had been attached to it.

At the flat that afternoon I was feeling a little better about myself, tidying up after the others and preparing clothes for work early the next morning, when there was a knock on the door. Leila's boyfriend, whom I had not previously met, had come to take her to a nearby hotel for a few drinks, but she wasn't home yet. I let him wait in the lounge room, and heard him use the phone to call her workplace. Soon he came to the kitchen door where I was washing dishes to ask me to tell Leila to meet him down at the hotel.

Another hour or so passed and he was back, asking if Leila had arrived. As she was still not home he said he'd go back to the hotel and if she did not join him within an hour, would I tell her that he'd gone home. I went back to my chores.

The first notion I had that something was wrong was

the sound of glass breaking in the lounge room. I ran out to see what it was. Leila was there, her face darkened with rage, a vase from the table in fragments on the other side of the room. Water and flowers completed the mess on the floor.

'Slut!' she began. I was startled and had no idea what she was raving about. Her anger spilled out as she swept everything from the table and mantelpiece onto the floor. 'You slept with him.'

'With who? What are you talking about?' I asked, completely bewildered. I had not even given her the message yet.

'Well, you can have him. You'll make a fine pair. I don't want a cripple anyway. Him and his withered little arm!' I hadn't looked at her visitor closely enough to notice anything unusual about him. I quickly told her he was waiting at the hotel and if she hurried she'd catch him before he went home.

Instead, she dashed into the kitchen and came back with a large, shiny knife. She looked totally deranged and I quickly put the table between us. When she began circling it, making sweeping motions with the knife, so did I, then I tried to make a dash to the door.

'I'll kill you. You don't deserve a child. It should be me with the baby, not you, you slut.'

I realised now that she was crazy, something had happened that day which had made her snap, or she may have been drinking or taken some sort of drug. I sprinted towards the door and the knife sailed by me, clattering against the wall and falling onto the floor.

Outside the house, down the stairs and into the street, my heart pounding. I ran until I reached a park nearby, where I climbed up into the stout branches of a tree. From there I could see the entrance to the duplex in which we lived. Eventually, since Leila did not emerge, my adrenalin level subsided and I started to wonder what next? Now what? Where do I go from here?

Hours passed, houselights in the street began to go off, and still I crouched on my perch in the tree. At last, legs aching from their cramped position, I slid down the trunk. Stealthily, I crept back up the hill, around to the back of the block of flats. The kitchen door was unlocked and I tiptoed in. The door to Leila's room was closed. I didn't want to risk her perhaps hearing me, running out and starting up all over again, so I just picked up my shoulder bag and left the way I had come in. I didn't know where I was going as I knew no one else in Sydney.

The thought that I had a job to start at 6.30 next morning became my focus. I had enough small change to catch a bus into town—if they were still running. I hoped to find an all-night cafe in which to wait safely, then go to my workplace early, wash and change into the pastel uniform with which I'd been provided.

I found a cafe not far from Central Railway Station. It catered to the odd assortment of characters who frequent such places late at night, some slightly crazy and talking to themselves, bent over their coffee cups. The couple who worked there also served travellers and those who had missed the last train and were forced by circumstances and poverty to hang around until the morning. The couple did not appear to think there was anything odd about a slight Black girl buying a cup of coffee and propping a tattered novel up on the sugar bowl. Compared to some of the unkempt, grubby and smelly men seated around me, snoring in their chairs with their heads against the wall, I probably looked downright ordinary.

I wasn't really reading but nor was I asleep when a thin young man about my own age and cleanly if plainly dressed slid into the bench on the other side of my table. He had a steaming cup of coffee in his hand and asked if I minded his sharing my table.

We struck up a conversation and soon I was telling him of my most immediate woes. He was solicitous and told me he had a tiny room in a building on William Street, leading up to Kings Cross. It was very plain, he said, but preferable to sleeping in a cafe. It only had one single bed, but he had extra blankets and he was willing to sleep on the floor, no strings attached.

His door opened directly onto the street and from inside the room I could hear the occasional sound of footfalls as people walked past on the footpath. There were no extra blankets but he piled up his clothes and slept on them, with a greatcoat spread over him to keep himself warm. Through cracks in the wall and around the door, street lighting lit the room even when the single light bulb was turned off. He wound his clock and set the alarm to wake me in three hours time, when I had to go to the hospital. Exhaustion knocked me out.

On my first day I found that another Black woman also worked in the hospital dining room. She was from an island in the Pacific, some place I had never heard of. We worked broken shifts—breakfast, lunch and tea. As soon as I'd established what my schedule was to be, I used the longest break to return to Leila's flat and collect my suitcase. One of the other women was home and let me in. She and the other woman living in the flat were almost like strangers to me. I said nothing about what had transpired between Leila and myself, and the woman didn't show any interest in my absence or my sudden departure.

Leila had gone through my suitcase and removed everything she'd fancied, but there had been little of value to take as I owned virtually nothing. I was very annoyed that she'd stolen the photos of my son, but not angry enough to stay and confront her about it. Leila was a good four inches taller and several stone heavier than me; she could have picked me up by my scrawny neck and choked the life out of me if she felt so inclined. Flight seemed the smartest, if not the bravest, option.

I was soon to discover that the poorest people have a greater sense of caring for strangers than anyone else I have ever met. Despite having so little themselves, they look out for and respond to need.

Finishing up my last shift for the day, I found myself outside the hospital with my suitcase in my hand, a few coins in my pocket and nowhere to go. The Black woman told me that she had friends we'd run into on William Street who were bound to know what I should do. We also ran into the young man who had, with great chivalry, given up his bed for me the night before. With two shillings from here, another from there, and advice about where a clean room costing one pound seven and sixpence a week had recently been vacated, I was soon the proud occupant of a very tiny attic in Victoria Street, Kings Cross. The ceiling sloped sharply so that I could only stand upright on one side of the narrow room, but it had the luxury of the smallest refrigerator I had ever seen and I felt like a queen. The gift of a battered half-pint saucepan enabled me to heat water or cans of baked beans on a gas ring in the kitchenette one floor below, but the most precious present of all that I received at this time was the unquestioning friendship from the people I met.

They were all young, none more than about twenty years old. Most, like me, could fit all their worldly possessions into a suitcase, though some did not even own a suitcase. In the many long talks we shared, I learned that they all had aspirations, all wanted to do something better with their lives, had an eye on the future, and each had a story of family disintegration or alienation which had to a very large extent determined their present circumstances. However, despite their frankness with me, I felt unable to share my own story. Instead I picked out bits and pieces to tell them when it became my turn to speak. The secret pain I carried was still too raw, too ugly, too heavy, for me to lay at another's door. Thus began my year of living dangerously.

My path home from Sydney Hospital took me past a discotheque, then known as Sound Lounge, which my new Black friend had taken me to one night after work. It became the centre of my life. Scarcely a night went by without me slipping in there and dancing myself into a state of exhaustion, before going home to sleep. It was, I found, a very good way of keeping the demons at bay, of preventing myself from going into 'shocks'.

My frenzied rhythmic dancing, with which I had already won applause and competitions in Townsville, transformed me and I spent as much time dancing as I possibly could. Soon the manager of a Kings Cross nightclub asked me if I would be interested in dancing on stage and being paid to do so. I couldn't believe it. And when he said that I'd be paid more than double what I earned carrying plates backwards and forwards at the hospital, I thought I was having a fantasy. Because my life had been so unsettled I had been unable to write to my previous employers for copies of my references. Carrying dishes had begun to look like being my entire life.

It was not until I had given notice at the hospital that I learned there was a catch to the offer to dance. The costume I was to wear was brief. By today's standards it would be considered seriously over-dressed for work on the stage, but at the time any skimpy costume was generally thought to be downright immoral. Police came into the clubs from time to time with tape measures to ensure that the sides of the bottom of women's two piece costumes were no narrower than four inches. In these days of the string bikini, see-through clothes and topless beaches, the norms of the early 1960s seem ludicrous in retrospect. Still, even at the time New South Wales laws were considered progressive when compared to Victoria, where hotels closed at 6 pm and no alcoholic beverage could be served without being consumed with a meal after that hour.

I wasn't particularly happy about dancing around on a stage in a brief costume with everyone in the audience, fully dressed, watching, and my attitude showed. Another entertainer, Kahu, a Maori who used fire and snakes in his acts, took me under his wing. He suggested I include a snake in my own performance and I nearly fell off my chair. Why hadn't I thought of this myself? After all, my totem is the snake and I got along with them very well.

Under Kahu's guidance I bought a large python from a pet store near Central Station, made an appropriate costume which couldn't snag on the snake's skin and had a wooden case made in which to carry the snake from one venue to another, with a fine brass gauze panel installed in the top so it could breathe.

Kahu became a special friend to me, perhaps because he, too, was a long way from home and knew about depression and isolation. Also probably because we were two dark-skinned people trying to survive in the otherwise very white and quite closed world of entertainment. The other Black entertainers we saw were Americans—big-name stars visiting Australia for a few days to perform at expensive venues, such as Chequers, the Chevron Hotel and other classy nightclubs. They were often surprised to see our brown faces in their audience and some came out front after their shows to talk with us. A few even came to watch Kahu's performances or to sit around and chat. I particularly remember Earl Grant because he perched on my snake box when he joined us as there weren't enough chairs. After half an hour or so someone at our table told him that his uncomfortable seat was a snake carry-case. In disbelief he bent down and peered through the shiny panel, then let out a scream and went running up the stairs and into the street. We didn't see him back there that night.

Kahu was the first man I had met who could cook and sew. He kept his tiny flat immaculate and I was always a welcome guest. On what could have been the loneliest day of my life, Christmas Day 1961, in the late morning Kahu sent two of his friends to rouse me from my bed and bring me to his place for lunch and a small festive celebration. I was so overwhelmingly grateful for his concern for me that my tears threatened to ruin the day until he took me aside and said, 'We're all in the same boat here, all alone, and we all look out for each other. I cooked. Your job is to smile.' He had the capacity to make the complexity of life seem quite simple.

Over time I had several rock pythons, carpet and diamond snakes come to live with me. I named them, depending upon their gender, Lucifer, Satan, Diablo, Delilah and Jezebel, reflecting the way society reacts to these beautiful but largely unknown and unloved creatures.

Snakes provided me with personal security. As well as carrying them around with me in their box, I put up mesh on the windows and gave them free rein in my apartment. I often wore them under my coat, draped around me, and I would bring them to parks for sunshine and air, and the chance to climb in the trees. The snakes, like me, were from the north and unused to being in an urban environment. I took them mainly to Rushcutters Bay Park to start their training and get them accustomed to being handled. Snakes are used to having their ten and twelve-foot long bodies almost completely supported along their length. Each one, therefore, required a great deal of love and patience to develop sufficient trust to allow it to be held aloft with only my hand beneath it for support.

To gain the snake's trust I would let it slide across my hand on the ground and lay there, then successively raise my hand a little higher, until at last the snake would have only its head and tail on the ground, the bulk of its body supported by my hand. It often took weeks to get this far. When at last I felt we were both ready, I'd raise the snake that last little bit further, and if my intuition was correct, the snake would allow itself to stay suspended for a few minutes. If not, the creature would whip its head and tail frantically and lash itself around me, struggling for purchase, sometimes almost strangling me in the process!

The snake was happier to be worn when I was out walking than to be carried in its box. It would cling to me with the minimum strength required to hold itself in place, wound two or three times around my waist. If I stopped along the way to have a coffee or chat, however, it would squirm around to see why we'd come to a halt. Snakes love warmth but are unable to generate their own heat, so it's easy to see why they are so happy to nestle against a warm body.

Snakes do not hear but they pick up vibrations—and there aren't too many vibrations in their natural habitat. So exposure to loud music was another source of anxiety for them until they became used to it.

Because of my experience, and although I struggled against it, being out on the street, especially at night, made me very fearful. With my snakes, however, I felt much more in control since most people are afraid of snakes and know very little about them. On my occasional dates with men, for instance, it was not difficult to manoeuvre the outing to finish up at my place, where, of course, my snake would be just where I wanted it, waiting for me inside the door. In winter I'd leave the radiator on and thus be assured that it would be curled up in front of it. In summer, a baby's bath weighted down with a few inches of water in the bottom of it had the same effect—snakes love to lay in cool water on a very hot day. Otherwise the snake could be found in warm places, such as on top of my refrigerator or water heater. Men invited in for a coffee after an outing were usually on edge and anxious to leave at the earliest opportunity as soon as they realised we had company, that is if they didn't go screaming up the hall and out of the building as soon as I opened the door. I was asked to leave quite a few apartment buildings because of men screaming on their way out.

By accident, therefore, I had found the perfect way to keep men at arm's length. Rapists or potential suitors, they were all the same to me. Emotionally I was badly damaged and needed time to heal. I was not ready to get involved in relationships of a sexual nature. My lack of interest in men in this way was a source of curiosity and sometimes mirth to my small circle of friends, who nicknamed me 'Capon'—a desexed chicken. A couple of women who referred to themselves as 'camp' picked up on my disinterest in men, but I had no interest in sex with them either, though one in particular made a tremendous effort to befriend me. She always seemed to arrive at one of my favourite haunts just before me and arrange for the staff to have the strains of 'I want to be Bobby's girl' playing as I walked in.

I had moved from Victoria Street, Kings Cross into a variety of bedsitters and flats, including a period living in the Tor, a large old castle that housed entertainers, writers and eccentrics. It had seen grander days and been subdivided into huge rooms-to-let.

Leila knew the area where I was living and started hanging around Kings Cross and trying to get into my group of friends by telling them she was my sister. I was extremely unamused. She managed to pick up people who I knew only slightly, and I was forever being given messages from her. I met two Canadians, Buddy and Jimmy, who Leila latched on to, initially as a channel to pass on titbits of irrelevant information to me. However, when she broke into their boarding house and stole some of their musical equipment and cameras, she became more than just a nuisance.

One morning I was walking along Darlinghurst Road and the proprietor of a small cafe was standing in his doorway. He greeted me and cheerily told me that he had given my 'sister, Leila' a loan to enable her to fly to Townsville and bring back her son. My blood ran cold. Leila had shown him a photo. When he described the child, I knew it was *my* son, Russel, who she was talking about and that the photo was one of those she had stolen from my suitcase.

I ran to the nearest post office and hastily wrote a note to Mum. Although I had told Mum what I was doing and how I was making a living, and sent her money for Russel, I had not written to her about the drama that had occurred between Leila and myself. My message to her was brief: *I am concerned for Russel's life and safety. Please do not leave him alone with Leila for any reason. Do not let her take him out anywhere. I'll write a longer letter later to explain.* I sent it off airmail express and special delivery.

My concern that Leila intended to abduct Russel was well founded, but Mum was alerted and no opportunity arose. I had begun to suspect that Leila was taking some sort of drugs, a guess based on the company I had heard she was being seen with. She returned to Sydney but did not pay back the cafe proprietor's 'loan', a fact he apprised me of from time to time. Instead of moving back to the Coogee flat she briefly took a room in Kings Cross.

I next heard that Leila had gone to work at a hospital somewhere around Surfers Paradise. I felt relieved as she was a threat to me in so many ways—embarrassing me by telling people she was my sister in order to get close to them, then stealing from them, telling lies, not to mention the physical threat that she posed.

When I learned that she had gone, I arranged for Russel to spend a few weeks with me.

What a lovely time we had together! He was about eighteen months old and full of mischief, and his stunning looks turned heads. However, he wasn't very interested in learning to talk as he could get anything he wanted by pointing and raising his expressive face towards any adult within cooee. What money I had I squandered on him, buying him a wardrobe of little Italian shoes and dapper clothes. When he returned to Townsville, Mum wrote to me: 'He went to Sydney a baby and came back a little man.'

A few weeks after Russel had gone home, I answered a knock at the door to find a man from the government welfare department standing in the hall. He had come, he said, to inspect my flat and ask me some questions, having learned that I had a child with me. He looked around my small but spotless flat, even though I told him that my son had returned to North Queensland. When I offered him a cup of tea he accepted and, more relaxed now, became quite chatty. He explained that it was his job to remove children from unsuitable premises and family situations, and that a large number of these removals were 'dark' children. They were sent to homes, he said, and some were adopted out.

Towards the end of his visit he assured me that, since Russel was no longer with me, I would not be bothered again. As I was seeing him out, I asked him who had drawn the attention of the department to me. 'Your mother,' he said. I was shocked. How could she have done this, I wondered, after all the trouble she had had from the welfare when I was a child? Much later, when I was again living in Townsville, I told her about this caller and asked why she had done it. 'I wrote to ask them to look at your place,' she said, 'because I couldn't get down there to see for myself,' as if this response was completely self-explanatory.

Not long after Russel went home Mum wrote to me of Leila's death. Like her mother before her, Leila had committed suicide. Following her many attempts over the years, she had finally succeeded. But, Mum said, at the last minute, as the emergency staff were pumping the pills out of her stomach yet again, she had changed her mind and begged them to save her. Her father, Laaka, was broken-hearted as Leila was his only child. 'She has gone to a peace,' Mum wrote, 'that she was never able to find on this earth.'

Despite Russel's recent visit and the veneer of exuberance that permeates the entertainment industry, I envied Leila in the peace of complete oblivion.

Mum's regular correspondence kept me informed about some of the events happening in Townsville and with the movements of my sisters. In my early teenage years, two brothers had, for a time, hung around in our area and visited us at our house. The elder, Bobby, was tall, dark-haired, good-looking, articulate and bright; the younger, Barry, was much fairer and a little slower, physically and mentally. He was always lagging behind, and we called him DK, which meant 'Dumb Kid', even though he was a little older than Dellie and me. The brothers had been around for a short while and then disappeared, as youthful friends seemed to do. We had never been very close and I had all but forgotten them.

Out of the blue I received an extremely angry letter from Mum telling me that 'your friend, Barry Hadlow, has committed a heinous crime'. He had raped and murdered a five-year-old girl and hidden her body in the boot of a car. This was in November 1962. When her parents had reported her missing and a search had been mounted, Barry had joined the search parties, but eventually he was charged with the crime. Perhaps Mum used her letters to vent the repugnance which all Townsville residents, indeed people everywhere, feel towards this type of crime, but it seemed terribly unjust to slant it somehow towards me—claiming that he had been *my* friend, instead of someone who was just about the place when I was thirteen.

Following her letter I endured a period when I had very short, troubled sleep and suffered recurring nightmares in which this poor raped and murdered child and I were constantly changing places. I would wake screaming and sweating profusely, from a dream in which I was trapped in the boot of a car. 'Let me out, let me out, I'm not dead,' I yelled in my sleep, yet, awake, I often wished that I was the one who was dead.

A few years later, Barry's brother, Bobby Hadlow, stopped me in the street. I told him how surprised I was that he would dare to speak to me in view of what his brother had done, but I joined him for a cup of coffee. His brother, he said, had enlisted in the Army and had been shot in the head during training on the rifle range. A metal plate had been inserted in his head, and he'd been discharged a completely different person from the one I had known. He was so odd even his family didn't know him. The court had disallowed evidence regarding this accident to be admitted during the trial and the Army had refused to release information about it. Bobby and his family were devastated by everything that had happened, but the streets were a safer place with Barry, so severely mentally damaged, not walking along them, Bobby said. Although, he would have preferred Barry to be in a hospital rather than a prison.

I was learning more about the awful things that can go wrong in this life, and that such a series of tragedies had touched people I knew made me feel both afraid and reckless. What meaning did life have, if things can go wrong at any time, regardless of our own best efforts?

Some time later I was again walking down Darlinghurst Road when I experienced an overwhelming urge to go into a newsagency and buy a newspaper. I regularly bought the *Australasian Post* for its giant crosswords, but apart from that my reading consisted of fiction and non-fiction books. The feeling that I must buy a paper was surrounded by other sensations I had experienced when I was receiving paranormal messages: light-headedness, no thoughts other than the direction I was somehow being given, and an urgency and anxiety about the mission that caused me to do it immediately in order to alleviate my distress about it.

Running home with the paper in my hand, I was very hot and bothered, though there had been nothing in the headlines to alarm me. I couldn't imagine what would have any significance for me in the paper. But as I flicked through its pages, moving towards the centre where news items grew smaller and smaller, the paper itself became warmer and warmer. When I arrived at that page which it was obviously my destiny to read, the paper felt positively hot. There, a tiny paragraph, a bare few lines, informed me that a child had been killed in a bicycle accident in Newcastle. I read it over two or three times, trying to work out its meaning, before it hit me. The child's surname, Appleby, was the name Mum had told me was the surname of my brother, the child

Mum had given birth to and reared almost twenty years before I was born. From somewhere deep in my memory, I recalled that my brother Jimmy lived in Newcastle, though I had never known his address. Certainly it hadn't occurred to me when I was staying with Skip's relatives in Newcastle. I was filled with the certainty that in my hand was a notice of the death of my nephew, a child I hadn't known existed.

I immediately mailed the clipping to Mum. I knew such a small item of New South Wales news would never make it into the *Townsville Daily Bulletin*, and she would be unlikely to find out otherwise. She had lost all contact with her son, James. Strangely, while Mum responded to the little note I included, she didn't mention that she'd received the clipping. What grief she felt, she bore in silence.

I continued to meet with my two Canadian friends. Buddy was excited at the prospect that his wife, Brunie, would soon join him, although I noticed that his friend, Jimmy, did not seem as pleased. Perhaps he regarded her arrival as a dampener to their mateship and running around together. We three had met for breakfast at a tiny cafe in a sidestreet in the Cross and, after ordering, Jimmy walked around the corner to buy a newspaper. When he returned he was deeply distressed and told us, and everyone else within earshot, that President Kennedy had been shot.

Although not a close follower of politics at the time, either here or overseas, I knew who President Kennedy was. Buddy, Jimmy and I had talked about the wind of change that we felt his youthful presence in the White House signalled. We were all thunder-struck, and spent the next few days huddled together, supporting each other through the shock, because the safety of everyone in the entire world now seemed to be under threat. This experience gave us a common bond, and we remained friends for several years.

I had met a wide variety of people by living and working in Kings Cross: business people, crooks, sharks, gamblers, hoons, standover merchants, as well as poets, painters and artists. Rosslyn Norton, or Rowie as she was called, was a Kings Cross identity who was commonly considered to be a witch. I didn't meet her— she once sent me a gift of a dead toad in a shoebox and had stood outside the window of my first-floor flat in the night, yelling out that she loved me. After that I made sure I never met her.

Despite my work in the entertainment industry where the demands are for laughs and smiles, I remained a very serious person. Between shows I sat in the dressing rooms, reading books and doing my *Australasian Post* crossword puzzles, to which I was virtually addicted, while the other performers circulated amongst the patrons, encouraging them to buy expensive drinks and sometimes arranging to meet them after the show. From time to time unknown fans sent champagne and imported boxes of chocolates backstage to me via the waiters. At first I sent them back, but the other women became cross, telling me that women with any class at all *do not* refuse expensive gifts. My ways, I must confess, did not endear me to some of the other performers, who often jibed me, saying I was dull, even though I gave them my gifts of champagne because I didn't drink.

After work, while others dressed glamorously and went off to nightclubs, I put on my tights, long jerkin and flat dancing shoes and went down to the Sound Lounge. There, from about midnight, I held impromptu dance classes for prostitutes who had just finished work. It was not unusual for me to put in three or four hours of near solid dancing, pausing to sip orange juice or to run to the women's toilet when it was reported to me that one of my 'charges' had passed out there from taking amphetamines. Once Adrian Keefe, the sound operator, passed out from drugs and I employed my nursing skills to help him too.

My time at the Sound Lounge was spent helping the girls of the night feel better about their own bodies, after they had been abusing them all evening. I would encourage everyone to get up and move rhythmically to reach a state of exhaustion, after which, I thought, we could all go home and have a peaceful sleep without the need for any form of sedation.

Eventually the petty jealousies amongst some of the other performers at one of the clubs I worked in festered. I found some of my costumes shredded with a razor in the dressing room on the night before I was to audition for a new job. I found cigarettes dropped into cold drinks which I had left in my cubicle, and once the word 'Nigger' was written in lipstick on my makeup mirror. No one would own up to writing it or to seeing anyone else do it.

I left the clubs and went to an agent to find work. This meant carrying my costumes, snake box and music with me to a new venue each night, and not everywhere provided the luxury of a dressing room. At some venues I found that performers had to prepare for their act in the ladies' rooms shared by the patrons, and it was often difficult to secure my purse or valuables in those places. The work was not steady, and I was staggered to learn that some agents dole out jobs on the basis of which of their clients gives them the most expensive gifts. The irregularity of shows and the very moderate fees we were paid often barely covered rent, food and the few pounds' remittance I tried to send my mother, without the whole operation being contingent upon my showering agents with presents.

The regular exercise of dancing had contributed to my physical growth and general look and feeling of good health. Since Russel's birth I had grown three inches taller and, for the first time in my life, weighed in at more than seven stone. The switch from being a club employee to working through an agent, however, had a negative effect on me as I began to worry and skip meals in an effort to meet my commitments. Mum wrote that I wasn't to panic if I sometimes couldn't send any money—she said there was always enough in her house to feed one small child—but the feeling of responsibility rested heavily upon me.

Then I fell ill. I had been moving around, seeking always cheaper but still clean accommodation in an effort to make do, and at the time of falling ill I lived in a private hotel in Potts Point. As well as security, these quarters had the added advantage of having a switch-board to take messages for me from my agent, relieving me of the need to pay for a phone. But I had to bundle my snakes into the wardrobe twice a week when the housemaid came to clean the room and change the linen.

When the illness didn't pass, I went to see a doctor. After he examined me and found nothing physically wrong to cause such distress and lethargy, he began to ask questions about my life and state of mind. Instead of answering him, much to his astonishment I burst into tears.

'I want you to see a specialist,' he told me when my

grief had subsided, and he wrote out a referral. A few days later I took a bus into the city to find the Macquarie Street address he had carefully written on the envelope. I was dismayed when I reached the building to find the specialist's name on a brass plaque with 'Psychiatrist' stamped under it. I was sure I had some physical complaint, some parasite perhaps which had invaded my intestines, so to find that the doctor had sent me off to a shrink greatly disturbed me.

Still, as I had found it an effort to reach the surgery I decided I shouldn't waste the trip. After I had registered my attendance with the receptionist, I asked to use the ladies' room. In the privacy of the cubicle I carefully opened the referral letter and prepared to leave if its contents alarmed me. Instead, the few lines contained a request for the doctor to talk with me as the referring doctor suspected I had deep concerns, the nature of which he personally had been unable to determine.

The psychiatrist was a man of middle age, or so it appeared to me at the time. His dark hair showed wisps of grey although his face seemed youthful. After making a few preliminary notes on his pad, he turned his full attention to me and began to ask some very general questions. What did I do for a living? Was I in touch with my parents? Then he asked if I was happy. His question seemed so terrible that I was completely unable to answer. After a few moments of silence I felt tears welling up in my eyes and to my great embarrassment I began to weep quietly. I could not stop the tears flowing down my face. He got up and snibbed the lock on his door, came back and put what he may have hoped was a reassuring hand on my shoulder. I flinched.

He took his cue from my reaction and went back behind his desk; the distance and barrier made me feel a bit safer. In a sort of shorthand I told him I had been the victim of a crime in which a large number of men had raped and tried to kill me, and that there had been many court cases. His eyes opened wide, though not in disbelief, and he was obviously aghast by what I was saying.

Eventually he said that he didn't think he could help me, that I didn't need and possibly couldn't afford psychiatric help, and that I would find that time would prove to be the greatest healer. I went home feeling quite stunned, suspecting that perhaps I was *so* crazy that even a psychiatrist couldn't help me. I lived through the next few days in a haze, so filled with self-doubt I could barely function.

I was more than a little surprised when, about a week later, the psychiatrist sent me a message asking me to phone him. When I did so his receptionist put me through to him immediately. He asked if I would like to meet him for a coffee. I was wary and agreed to meet him, but not for coffee. I was so suspicious of any sort of personal attention from a male that, away from the surgery, I would only speak with the psychiatrist in broad daylight and in a public place outdoors. We set up a meeting for an early afternoon at a bench in Rush-cutters Bay Park. He brought bottles of cool drink. I brought one of my snakes.

Altogether we met about five or six times. It was evident that what I had told him about myself at his surgery had deeply disturbed him and he was concerned that I may have felt fobbed off by him. In his role as 'friend', he thought we could just meet occasionally to chat about my life and what progress I might be making. He kept encouraging me to 'get back into life' and made suggestions about how I could do this. He was concerned about the huge gulf and contradiction between my career as an entertainer—apparently social, outgoing, gregarious—and the enormously isolated and pained soul I became off-stage.

Coincidentally, several other things of importance happened around this time. I was walking up the hill along Bayswater Road one day when I noticed a dress store, but it only had two frocks in it. One was stunning, and I peeped around the door to look at it more closely. A quite young and extremely handsome blond man sat behind the counter, sewing sequins onto some shiny fabric, and we started to talk. He told me he was Dutch and that his partner, also European, had gone overseas to visit his parents. This was his shop and in it he tailored very special and expensive outfits for wealthy women and prostitutes in the area. He was taken with my exotic looks, he said after a while, and wished to make me a dress, for free, to complement my style. I had been given a lot of guff from some of the entertainers with whom I had worked. They had tried to erode my self-confidence by telling me that I was 'unladylike', didn't do my hair properly, didn't wear enough makeup, and so on. So I was absolutely thrilled to hear this man who had such obvious dress sense and charm tell me otherwise.

We became friends and began to spend a lot of time together, laying about on the beach and meeting up with his friends for cocktails at the Quarterdeck Bar. He made me several items of beautiful clothing—fancy dresses and day frocks—always inspired by particular locations we visited. When I had a work engagement some of his friends, many of whom were employed in theatrical and other flamboyant professions, spent time making up my face and generally turning me out to look eye-catching.

We would often go to his tastefully decorated apartment, which was in a luxury block of units, and several times I stayed overnight. He missed his partner, he told me, and welcomed my company. We made up exotic recipes, he was an excellent cook, and listened to music and laughed a lot. He delighted in trying out new ideas and clothing on me. In his large and modern bathroom we took bubble baths together, and later we would both put on some of the glamorous nightwear he owned, and he'd hold me gently when we went to sleep.

This sexually non-threatening and emotionally rewarding relationship with a man went a long way, I feel, towards allowing me to reconsider the position of men in society and in my life. My psychiatrist friend encouraged me in this friendship, telling me that, although it didn't really fall into a 'normal' relationship between a man and a woman, the security and joy that it brought me was definitely very healthy and a step in the right direction.

Otherwise, my relationships with men remained dismal. I sought care, encouragement and emotional support, while the men I met were in a seemingly constant search for sex. Through my work I came into contact with a wide variety of men from all walks of life, and those exceptions who were not on the hunt were few and far between.

Kings Cross was a hub, a place where people who lived in the suburbs came to have a good time, even if they only made such an excursion once or twice a year to celebrate birthdays, anniversaries or promotions.

The streets teemed with people all night, and the dregs and stayers—women in bedraggled evening dresses and camp guys in women's clothes and five o'clock shadows, as well as straight men in a variety of guises—could always be seen limping home at dawn while street-sweepers and milkmen made their early morning rounds.

Cross-titutes, as people who lived in, rather than visited, the Cross used to call themselves, were also a very mixed bag. The area seemed to beckon to all manner of eccentrics, the rich and the poor, and Kings Cross garrets attracted artists, writers and others who wished to live close to the city and in the company of hopefully like-minded people.

I was walking into an expensive and popular nightclub in Darlinghurst Road one night to meet friends when I saw a short, swarthy and well-dressed man standing alone against a wall. He seemed to glower at me as I passed. When I joined my friends they remarked that they had watched him staring at me, and that I had better be on alert. His name was Abe Saffron. I had heard of his almost legendary reputation as a crime boss and owner of illegal gambling houses, as well as tales told by some of the entertainers about his brutal treatment of women. One woman had told me that she was his short-term 'girlfriend', 'the girlfriend you have when your real girlfriend is pregnant' she'd said. When Saffron discovered that she had been seen with some other man he had stood by while his thugs smacked her around so seriously that she had to be hospitalised. I strained in my chair to take a look at him. It was wise, I thought, to know what people look like if you want to avoid them.

Not too long after that I was hired to perform in a

small club in the southern suburbs on a Friday night. After completing the work, I packed up and went to collect my pay. The manager told me to go to a table in the back where 'a man will pay you'. This area of the club was poorly lit, in fact it was downright gloomy, and only by peering could I see a figure sitting alone at one of the tables. I was right up at the table before I realised the man was Abe Saffron. A crisp white envelope lay on the table between us, my pay. Mr Saffron nudged the envelope towards me, but as I reached for it, he lay his hand over it. I wished I was still wearing my snake, but I'd returned it to its box after the show and, with my costume bag, it was on the floor near the dressing-room door. Mr Saffron, however, couldn't have been more charming.

'I'd like to invite you to a party,' he said. His mouth was smiling but the geniality didn't reach his eyes.

'I'm sorry, but I'm expected somewhere else as soon as I finish here,' I replied.

'The party's *tomorrow* night.' The smile didn't leave his face. I could feel panic rise in my heart, and I was glad the room was dark enough for him not to see my alarm. I was lost for a rejoinder.

From his pocket he took a square of paper on which was written an address. He put the piece of paper on top of my pay envelope. I reached across and picked them both up, watching him watching me, feeling the tension like predator and prey. I had heard talk of his 'parties' and they didn't sound like somewhere I'd want to go, but I didn't feel I could say anything. His tone was more like an order than an invitation.

'Where are you going now? I'll give you a lift,' he said, and this time I was quick.

'My boyfriend is waiting for me in a car outside.'

'Well, I'll see you tomorrow night then. Goodnight.'

There was no boyfriend waiting for me, and I picked up my things and left by the back entrance. I ran down the stairs and into a dark suburban street, then around the block and back onto the main street. I thought it was too much of a risk to try to flag a cab there, still too close to the club, so I sat on my snake box in the dark around the corner from the highway and waited for an hour or so to pass, sweating about what I should do. As I didn't know the area I had no option but to stay where I was until I felt sufficient time had elapsed to make it safe for me to hail a taxi. I took Jezebel, my snake, out of her box and let her wind herself around me—just in case.

The following Tuesday I rang my agent to inquire about bookings, however, I was met with a strained silence at her end. 'Anything the matter?' I asked.

'Can you come in?' she replied.

Work for individual entertainers was often difficult to obtain. Clubs rang, wanting 'an act', 'a singer', 'a comedian'. Only rarely did they specify any particular act, so if agents asked you to stand on your head, most entertainers would try to oblige. And so it was that I found myself in her office, watching her flutter through sheafs of paper as she prepared herself to offload her problem.

'I don't know who you've offended or what you've done,' she at last said, 'but it's unlikely you'll get much work in this town now.'

'What?' I spluttered. 'What do you mean?'

'Well, let me put it this way. I can't give you any work.'

I reeled out onto the street and was dazzled by the brightness of the sunshine. Such a perfect looking day for something this bizarre to happen, I thought. I crossed Oxford Street and wandered into Hyde Park, needing a few minutes to comprehend this sudden news. So this was my 'punishment' for not turning up at Abe Saffron's party, I realised, and was angry. For Mr Saffron or whichever of his henchmen had called the agent, the action meant nothing at all. Like swatting a mosquito, they would probably never think about it again. But for me, it was monumental, a demonstration of the power of money and influence over the destiny of a tiny nobody just minding her own business, trying to stay alive and earn enough to keep herself and her son.

I had heard of other girls who had been starved of work, shut out of the industry. Some had gone back to live with their parents in the suburbs, others latched on to their boyfriends and convinced them they were ready to settle down, but a few had hung around until they reached the point of starvation, leaving themselves with few options but to debase themselves in front of whoever they'd upset, hoping for mercy, or move into prostitution. I would not allow any of these things to happen to me. It was time for me to go, but go where?

Melbourne, I decided over the next two days. I learned that, despite its rigid liquor laws, Melbourne had at least one club that hired entertainers, the Forbidden City. I would go there and ask for work.

I had no real ties in Sydney and, having acquitted my rent, I decided to take the train as soon as I was packed. One friend, Jan, was virtually the only person I told I was going. Also an entertainer, Jan was in desperate circumstances herself. After leaving one club job she could not find another and was behind in her rent, so she immediately said she wanted to come with me.

She lowered her suitcase to me from the first-floor window of her Victoria Street rooming house because she could not walk out with it past her landlord. We felt like two escapees on the run!

On the train our carriage had few other passengers, so I let Jezebel out of her case. I didn't like to keep her cramped for too long and the trip to Melbourne seemed endless. When we arrived, however, she didn't fancy getting back into her box so I had to wrap my coat around her and carry her in a taxi. We had the driver take us directly to the Forbidden City.

I have no idea what the staff thought about us at first. We tumbled, travel-worn, out of the taxi with suitcases, snake box, and a snake wrapped warmly in a big coat. We asked at the front office of the hotel for the entertainment manager. He came out, giving us a look of incredulity but wearing a warm smile, and introduced himself as Ray. I managed to get Jezebel back into her box and he invited us in to watch the show. The club served dinner and the show ran in two parts, the audience consisting of couples and mixed group parties who possibly thought the place gave their evening a nice up-market, slightly risque edge.

Ray was tremendously thoughtful. He realised we were all but broke and homeless, so he contacted people he knew, Mr and Mrs Hall, who ran a boarding house a few streets away in St Kilda. The boarding house seemed to cater almost exclusively to men—scientists and specialists going to and from Antarctic expeditions. Ray arranged with the Halls for us to fix up our rent after we received our first pay from the club.

Mr and Mrs Hall were an elderly, happily married couple who had had no contact with snakes before, and possibly none with a Black woman either. It seemed, however, that very little fazed them. They told me they were quite used to eccentrics. Who else but eccentrics opt to spend a year at the South Pole, snowed in and with virtually no contact with the outside world? The Halls seemed to quietly revel in the idea of meeting people from all walks of life, and they treated everyone well. I lived with them the entire time I was in Melbourne, and they were pleased to come when we invited them to see the show.

Their red-brick home was warm and amicable, and Mrs Hall made friends with Jezebel in no time at all. She delighted in telling her friends that she had two 'showgirls' and a snake living with her. At first, some of the lodgers from the men's quarters weren't too happy to have their meals with Jezebel around, but they settled down when they saw others stepping over her without any harm coming to them. As it was more difficult in Melbourne than it had been in Sydney to find mice to feed her, Mr and Mrs Hall suggested I buy a pair of mice and let them breed to provide a steady supply of food. This worked well until the lot of them escaped from a wooden box I kept in the bottom of the wardrobe. When I opened the cupboard I discovered they had nibbled their way through most of my underwear. Mrs Hall just laughed and said she'd ask Mr Hall to fit the box with a better lock.

I felt safe in Mrs Hall's house and even walking to the club. We usually caught a taxi home as it was often midnight, but on the few occasions when I walked, Jezebel's presence discouraged most people from coming too close. On sunny days I took her to the St Kilda pier and to parks around the area, so many people began to realise that when they saw me, my snake would not be far away.

I was yearning again to see Russel. I had been away from Townsville for almost a year and he had visited me only once during that time. Mum wrote that she had pictures of me up all around the house, and Russel would point and say, 'Mama'. She said there was no possibility that he would forget who I was, but doubt niggled at me.

Entertainers at the Forbidden City were not permitted to fraternise with guests, not that there were many unaccompanied men in our audiences anyway. In between shows we had a roped-off area at the back of the room where we were served dinner. I was therefore surprised one night when Ray asked me if I would agree to talk with a friend of his, a surgeon, someone he could personally recommend, who had asked to meet me. If anyone else had made such a request I would have refused, but I knew that Ray was entirely on the up and up. He was the ideal person to run an entertainment program, always working for the best interests of both patrons and staff.

Our meeting was brief. The man was clean cut and otherwise nondescript. After our introduction he invited me to join him for coffee at his house one night the following week. I looked over his shoulder and saw Ray nod.

On the night, the gentleman waited in the lobby for me to finish work and took me to a most elegant house with a sweeping driveway. Inside, lights burned and he left his car at the front step rather than drive into the garage. This action assured me that he intended to drive me home in the not too-distant future, and the presence of his housekeeper set my mind completely at rest. A pleasant, grey-haired woman, she brought in a tray with tea, coffee, warm scones, cream and jam. I was also offered an alcoholic drink from a huge cocktail cabinet which seemed to contain every type of drink one can imagine.

When we'd settled into the big leather chairs and exchanged general chit-chat, the doctor got down to business. He had reached an age, he said, when he was looking for a wife. His wife, he continued with a sweep of his arm, would have all this. Was I interested to hear more?

Curious was probably a better word. I had read fiction in books and magazines about completely improbable marriage proposals, and I felt that I'd somehow strayed into such a story. But no, the doctor explained, he led a busy life and was engrossed in his work, too busy to socialise, meet people and go out on dates. On the other hand, the idea of having a wife in his house to be the hostess for his occasional dinner parties, a companion to take holidays and travel with, was becoming increasingly appealing to him. He painted the life on offer as one of luxurious indulgence, and he wanted, he said, a woman of exotic looks and charm.

I had sat silently listening while he told me all this, and it hadn't really crossed my mind that he had asked me no questions about myself. I was just amazed by the whole strange scene. However, his next words rang my alarm bells.

'I had a private detective checking up on you this past week,' he said, and added, 'I hope you don't mind.' I did mind. 'You come from Townsville, where your mother still lives, and you have two sisters. You are separated from your husband. I understand you have already had a child, a boy, who lives with your mother. Am I right so far?'

He had intruded on my personal territory and I was

aghast. I sat shocked. He didn't seem to notice and, in fact, appeared to be smug in his knowledge, as he continued, 'You don't smoke or drink, and you have no criminal record, and you have very good manners,' he said with a sort of smile, no doubt hoping to be reassuring.

Instead of feeling comforted by this positive assessment of my behaviour, my stomach wrenched. How could anyone, especially a complete stranger, without my knowledge or consent, gather information about me and sail so close to my secret. During the remainder of his talk with me he inferred that Skip was negligent, which I understood to mean that he thought he was the father of the child.

Drained by this encounter, coming as it did at the end of a long day and an evening at work, I began to make motions to leave. The housekeeper had disappeared after she had brought in the tray, but I had not heard a car start up so I guessed that she lived in. I was becoming distraught, not about his physical presence but because he had stirred my mind with his detective's report and his presumptuous manner.

Immediately, he became the concerned host and hastened to take me back to Mrs Hall's. I was not surprised that I didn't have to give him the address. Outside the house, where he pulled up and kept the engine gently purring, he asked me to consider going home to talk to my mother about his proposal. He had already outlined a long-term plan, which included a divorce that he would pay for, a diamond ring, which he would purchase six months after the divorce, and intervals at which he would begin putting things in my name if I went along with the plan. The whole idea consisted of a very detailed proposition, and he had obviously spent time and effort working it out. He said he would be happy to finance the trip to Townsville and this would incur no obligation for me to decide in his favour.

In bed that night I came to the conclusion that this meeting had been one of the weirdest things that had ever happened to me. The man had made no effort to touch me, did not so much as even accidentally touch my hand. At the time, I did not think that he may have been camp and was trying to establish a front for himself. Although, still puzzling over it years later this did occur to me as a possibility.

I didn't take the money he offered for a plane ticket, but I did use the idea of a trip home to see my mother and son as a means to justify leaving. I knew I had no intention of accepting his offer—I was too outraged by his employment of a private detective to check up on me to even consider it. But at the same time, I was somehow flattered. Someone had thought of me as a potentially good wife and partner. This was a far cry from the unhappy circumstances of my marriage to Skip, where his father had offered me money to disappear.

I said my goodbyes to Ray and the Halls, and set off again by train.

3

En route home to Queensland, I arranged to break the trip at Newcastle. During the first few months following my departure from Townsville, Mum had kept me informed of Skip's whereabouts. At first he had continued working for Hornibrooks, staying at her house on his days off, and he had teetered between wanting me to return and give our marriage another try, and cutting ties with me altogether. I'd asked Mum not to give him my address. She had written that several times he had given her money to send me to use to come home, then taken it back again after a few days. Sometime later he returned to Newcastle. I thought I would stop by there in an effort to finalise things between us.

Jezebel had been showing signs of illness just before I left Melbourne. On one occasion I had put a tiny live mouse into her carry basket for her to devour—she liked to catch her own food—but when I looked in later, I was dismayed to find that, instead of the snake eating the mouse, the mouse had nibbled some of the scales off Jezebel's back. I put cream on her wounds but I was more worried about her lack of appetite and vigour. But who could I call?

As soon as I arrived in Newcastle I phoned a well-known snake farm in the area and asked for some expert advice. Look in her mouth, I was told, and see if she has canker. Sure enough, I saw the telltale symptoms the man was describing to me. He then told me to give her a certain medication. When I walked into the nearest chemist shop with Jezebel wrapped in a shawl, the chemist scrambled up onto shelves at the back of his store. I apologised and said the snake was ill and wouldn't, couldn't, hurt him. Nevertheless, he preferred to remain there and he gave me directions to locate the ointment I needed. Then I rang up the purchase on his till, took the change and left. When I looked back he was climbing gingerly down.

Despite my letter and subsequent phone call, during which Skip had sounded enthusiastic about seeing me, he failed to meet with me during my stopover. I was disappointed but not surprised. My time there had been well spent gaining advice and medication for Jezebel. I caught the next train to Brisbane where Jezebel and I spent the day at Aunty Glad's before resuming our long journey.

At home in Townsville I found that Arthur had moved his barber shop out of the poolroom to a shopfront along Flinders Street, and that he and Mum, and whoever else they could get in to help, were running a hamburger store in the shop next door. They had put beds in the rooms at the back of the store, plus a cot for Russel to take a nap in during the day.

Jezebel caused a minor kerfuffle when I first introduced her, but everyone soon settled down when they saw how tame she was. I kept her in her basket at night but during the day she was given free reign throughout the back of the shop. One night she crept out of the basket and disappeared. We couldn't find her any-where, and I was afraid someone may have seen her outside and, in needless panic, killed her. She was over ten feet long so the first sight of her often alarmed people. We put a sign up in the front window, offering a reward for a sighting. A photographer from the *Townsville Daily Bulletin* arrived to take a photo of the sign, but otherwise we received no response. Fortu-nately, two days later we found her. She had wriggled up, or perhaps down, a drainpipe on the outside of the shop. Again I put her in her basket at night, but she'd discovered how to push open the lid so there was no keeping her still. I resorted to putting her in her wooden box at night, for fear that she'd frighten some-one and be killed as a result.

Perhaps my treatment of her canker was inadequate, or maybe she had a mishap that I didn't know about, such as someone accidentally stepping on her, because after a few weeks she died. I had thought that she would enjoy the warmer environment of the north, as I did, and recover her old self again. I was very upset by her death and was surprised when even Mum shared my distress. Mum said she had never liked snakes until she'd met Jezebel, and that she'd grown used to her and liked having her around. She made people feel safe.

I had learned a great deal about the nature of society and the wide spectrum of the human condition after spending a year living in the south and working in the entertainment industry. I had not, however, found a place for myself in that society. I was very much a loner, often struggling against suicidal urges as a response to feeling worthless and unvalued, or as was often the case, when things looked impossible for me. Despite my own shaky survival on the stage, I had witnessed the racism and sexism which permeated that area of work, and did not feel that I wanted to continue in that direction. For a Black woman, the stage held no real future. Audiences wanted to watch me because of my 'exotic' looks and were amazed by my rapport with snakes, but no one wanted to hear what I was thinking. To me, dancing was a physical expression of my emotions, of my pain, as well as a means to release the tension created by my pain, but it was a way of maintaining, not of progressing. I felt the need to go forward, but to where? Also, I realised how deeply I had missed Russel. Mum's physical care for him was excellent but he was quickly growing and reaching the age where his character would need to be moulded. This, I thought, had to be *my* challenge. Although he had been thrust upon me the child was not to blame, and he had a right to his mother's care and attention.

As always, one was roped into work whenever they were around at Mum's, so Dellie, Leonie and I all took turns at running the shop, making the hamburgers and milkshakes, and doing the million other chores involved. One night when Dellie and I had just closed up the store, two youths came up and banged on the door. We were planning to go out to the Norgate, where young people hung out at night, so we didn't want to open the store after we'd locked everything up. We could hear the young men cursing us as we turned out the lights.

William Sykes, an Englishman, and his friend were on their way to Mt Isa to look for work. After his arrival

in Australia, William had been involved in a car accident, and they were making the trip with funds from his
small compensation settlement. He said they had
heard there was work aplenty out west, although conditions were harsh. After he recovered from being
snubbed at the hamburger shop, William and I hit it off.
When they were leaving to continue their journey, he
asked if I'd like to go along with them and I agreed.
Mum told me she had worked in the canteen at Mt Isa
before I was born, and she encouraged me to go
because she had enjoyed high wages and the different
lifestyle while she was there.

A bonus about living in Mt Isa was that William
agreed that Russel should be with me. William's friend,
however, found the work and rough conditions not to
his liking, and split. There was work, though it was hot
and tough, but the main problem was lack of accommodation. After living in a flimsy caravan for weeks,
William found a family with a very basic house that
they wanted to share as a means of halving their
expenses. I managed to find a job in a steam laundry,
where the work was hard and heavy, and the boss
cursed and constantly and crudely insulted the women
who worked for him. I stuck it out for as long as I could,
but when I thought about it, I weighed up my distress
at being abused daily, the cost of childcare for Russel,
and the difficulties involved in both of us getting to and
from work with just one car between us. The idea that I
should stay at home, keep house and look after Russel,
ferry William backwards and forwards to work, and use
the car to get to the supermarket from our inconvenient
location was not only wiser but economically sound
too.

William earned good wages as a painter, working on

the mine's tall chimney shafts. He enjoyed the feeling of freedom working in the open, as well as the sense of danger from working at such a great height. An adventurer, William and his friends went hunting at night and weekends, and he happily took to eating bush turkey and other local food.

Although racism was solidly entrenched in Mt Isa, I often had a hard time convincing William that this was the case. Camps sprang up around the town, and while whites sometimes lived in them, they were predominantly Aboriginal. I sometimes saw pencil-thin barefoot dark children in the streets, their eyes always cast down. Blacks, men or women, were rarely employed in the town, even in menial positions. The local newspaper always carried letters to the editor spelling out how offended some whites were by the sight of the poverty of the Blacks, as though it was their own fault they were so poor. Many hotels refused to admit Blacks, or had segregated areas where they could drink or buy a bottle. At the time Blacks were not permitted by law to drink alcohol, so the sales were illegal, although the publicans were not prosecuted.

After I left the steam laundry, I created a position of status for myself in Mt Isa by always dressing to the hilt. I'd sweep around the supermarket and dusty streets in high heels, wearing some of the elegant clothes that had been made for me by my camp friend in Sydney. I'd walk with William into segregated hotels, dressed to kill, causing every head to turn, and order vodka, with a glass of orange juice on the side, although I really didn't drink the former. It was just a small way for me to challenge the segregation laws. Once I even ordered a martini, which caused a stir, and, much to our mirth, I was eventually served something completely undrinkable with an olive and an onion in it.

The white family with whom we shared the house had some crude ways which I found unhygienic and offensive. The house was infested with rats, but rather than set traps our housemates left biscuits on the kitchen floor so that the rats would eat them instead of ransacking the supplies in the cupboards. They refused to believe that this practice attracted rats and was even fattening them up. The man was particularly uncouth, and thought it a great joke to fart loudly around the house, even in bed where, after he did so, he would forcibly hold his wife's head under the sheet. We could hear her screaming.

I found Mt Isa interesting, but not a place where I would have liked to spend the rest of my life. The last straw came for me when, late one night, Russel had a fever and was screaming in pain. He was usually such a good child that I knew something serious was wrong with him. We rushed him to the hospital where a nurse said she would fetch the doctor on duty, who was asleep in a back room. When she returned alone, she told us with embarrassment that the doctor refused to come out. It was obvious from her demeanour that she had told him the patient was black. William was livid but there was nothing he could do. The nurse suggested we give Russel aspirin, and apologised that she had none to offer us. By that time Russel was writhing and thrashing in my arms, tugging at his ears and banging his hands against his head. We paced the floor anxiously all night, trying to pacify the screaming child and worried that he would die. We even discussed making a dash to Townsville to get medical attention, but such a journey on the unsealed roads and bush tracks, which at the time was the state of the 'highway', would have taken too long and been far too risky.

Although Russel recovered over the next few days, William and I were galvanised into returning to Townsville. Within a week or so I took Russel to the Townsville General Hospital where he received a complete check-up. Peering into his ears the doctor asked, 'How long have his eardrums been perforated?'

I gave him a blank look.

'Oh, you'd know when it happened. He would have been screaming and banging his head!'

'Well, in that case, two weeks.'

Russel ran around the room while I told Mum about the doctor's discovery, then he climbed up onto my lap. I stroked his beautiful smooth brown skin and wept silently as I thought that this innocent little child had already become a victim of racism and medical neglect, and that neither William nor I had been able to prevent it. The diagnosing doctor had given me a list of things Russel would never be able to do as a result of his perforated eardrums, such as travel in unsealed planes or deep dive; anything that would put pressure on the drums. At three years old his life and its limitations were already being shaped by racism.

I had discovered a lot about William during this time, most of which was good. He was not a very complex man—gentle, hard working and basically honest. Although his formal education exceeded my own, he was not a keen reader, preferring to play card games or watch television. He was a very moderate social drinker with a hearty appetite for food. Also he had, I thought, a well-developed sense of 'family'. He was very attentive to my mother and they got on extremely well.

Mum had organised for us to move into Mrs Sullivan's old cottage, next door to the house I had grown up in. Lodgers were still living there, including Mum's old friend Nellie, whose sight had badly deteriorated and she was then on the old-age pension. William and I helped out in Mum's hamburger shop each day while William was looking for work, and he often went on errands for Arthur.

We had only been in Townsville a couple of weeks and were asleep in bed with Russel sleeping nearby, when the door to our bedroom burst open. Two detectives stood in the narrow hallway, with Nellie crying loudly behind them. She had heard them at the front door and when she'd opened it, they'd thrust their way past her, looking for William. The police hauled him out of bed and took him off to the police station.

I quickly dressed Russel and myself and drove down to Mum's shop. Police were swarming all over it, searching every nook and cranny. I told Mum that the police had William, and she said that she thought they were also arresting Arthur.

When William was finally released, without any charges being laid, he said the police had beaten him up. They had kept asking him what he was doing in a certain street in Railway Estate and what was it that he had put in the boot of his car at a house there. William was unfamiliar with Townsville, having spent only a short time there before, and although he could find his way from one place to another he'd not yet learned the names of streets. Arthur had asked him to pick up some milk crates from a building they had been to previously, and William could always find his way back to anywhere he had been before. The detectives may have thought he was being deceptive by claiming not to know the street they were talking about, but he wasn't.

I was cross when William was unwilling to make a complaint against the police beating him; his reluctance puzzled me. Throughout the troubling times following the rape in Brisbane and the subsequent trials it had been instilled in me that the role of the police was as protectors and law enforcers. Police who acted against the laws they were sworn to uphold had to be brought to account, at least in my mind. I understood by then that Arthur was dishonest and engaged in criminal stupidity, but William had done nothing except run an errand for Arthur. Merely by his association with Arthur he was assumed to be a criminal.

The police also searched Mum's house in Aitkenvale and found a starting pistol. It only fired blanks, a relic of Dellie's days as a successful track athlete. Nevertheless, the police arrested Mum and charged her. She went to court where she was treated lightly, but for years later, when she was in a good mood, we laughingly teased her for being a 'gun moll'.

During this time, as well as running the hamburger shop, Mum continued to work as a laundress at the Central Hotel, which was three blocks away from the shop along Flinders Street. She was exhausted, and at last she saw her way clear to slowing down a bit. She wanted me to take over the laundress job, and went ahead and arranged it with the manager even though I had not expressed any desire to do so. 'You need the money,' Mum said, 'so just do the work. It's not too heavy and the manager and his wife will leave you alone.'

The laundry was in a poky lean-to at the back of the hotel, with only a small window, and the appliances were primitive. Steam and fumes from the gas copper filled the room, along with the rank beer smell of bar towels. The ironing was done on an upstairs verandah, where at least one could catch the breeze coming off Ross River. I had occasionally relieved Mum at this job, and knew that I would be sick to my stomach with the smell of sour beer, but Mum persisted. What I hadn't told her was that even a wisp of this smell brought on 'shocks', flashbacks, as also happened when I smelled beer on anyone's breath. I was suddenly catapulted back into a dark shed, in great fear and struggling for my life.

During the short time I worked in the laundry, I constantly expressed my unhappiness, but Mum would hear none of it. 'You are making yourself unhappy,' she would often tell me. 'You think you are too good for that sort of work, and you're not. You have a child to support now, and you have to get any fancy ideas out of your head. Not many coloured women get the chances you've had, I can tell you!'

The 'chance' I had was to work in a sweathouse. I felt badly, because Mum had been doing the job for years. She had brought us up with the sweat from her brow and labour which had bent her body. I was disappointed that she didn't appear to want better for her own children. Her expectations were that I should follow in her footsteps. I didn't have dreams, but I had dreads, and slaving away without any opportunity to use my brain and test my potential was one of them.

A nice thing happened during this time. My Canadian friends, Buddy and Jimmy, moved to Townsville, along with Buddy's wife, Brunie, and their young daughter, Naomi. They were now involved in the Mormon Church, and I learned a lot from them about the Mormon philosophy. The more I learned, however, the less likely it became that I would ever join. Black people, so they informed me, could join the Church, but only at the very lowest level, where they would have to be content to remain. Their teachings were that being Black meant that the person had been very evil in their last life. White people had been good in past lives and being white was somehow their reward. I found the concept extremely racist and perhaps designed to force Blacks to accept a servile position in society, just as they were made to accept a lowly place if they wanted to be part of this Church. We often argued, and I wondered how they could be party to such a congregation yet accept me into their lives as a valued friend.

Brunie and I spent a lot of time together. She had shoulder length dark glossy hair and was extremely attractive. With glamorous clothes, she caught the eye of many men as we drove around town. I thought her very daring, and it was an adventure just to be in her company. She was an excellent seamstress and made many of the clothes she and her daughter wore, and she was happy to teach me to sew. We made ourselves twin outfits, two-piece white suits with piping on them, that we wore out together with great pride. William was happy enough when Brunie came to visit, but he didn't take a shine to Buddy or Jimmy, who were generally too busy with their Church duties to sit down and talk often, anyway.

A friend of William's who lived in Brisbane asked William to be his best man. Leaving Russel in Mum's care, we drove down for the ceremony. As was often the case, I was the only person of colour at this gathering of relations and friends, but I tried to be positive in my outlook towards everybody and hoped they would be likewise towards me.

At the reception, held in the groom's parents' house, I was appalled when the father of the groom came into the kitchen where I was washing dishes and tried to sexually molest me, calling me names when I resisted. Others heard him and came in to take him away, but I was very upset and didn't want to stay. William later told me that, during my absences earlier in the evening, when I had been preparing food and helping to clean up in the kitchen, he had been shocked by the attitude of his friend's father towards the idea that William and I were planning to marry. 'Have an affair with the darkies, by all means. But marry them? Never!' he had been advised.

Throughout our relationship I had a major problem with William's selective memory. I always had to keep in mind that racism was a fact of life, and therefore I had to learn ways to protect Russel and myself from this discrimination. William, however, preferred to forget about racism and discrimination, to block them out and pretend they never happened, and he expected me to do the same. Racism often surfaces in what may appear to be an unrelated series of events. Black people must look for this pattern of racism, otherwise they might feel that they themselves have done something wrong which warranted the abuse. Over time, this feeling completely destroys self-esteem, which is essential for one's happiness and success.

For a variety of reasons, including the distress caused by working at the Central Hotel, William and I were unable to settle down in Townsville. Much to Mum's annoyance, I gave notice and we packed up and moved to Brisbane. I applied to the Mater Hospital again, hoping there might have been an opening in the ante-natal clinic, but the hospital staff claimed they could find no record of my having worked for them before. Still without my nursing papers, they could only offer me cleaning work. As we were desperate for money, I accepted the position of kitchen-hand for a month, and found myself literally up to my elbows in grey washing-up water from dawn, cleaning huge cooking pots and pans that were too big to be put into the dishwasher. During my last week there, an elderly nun came through the kitchen and she stopped when she saw me.

'Haven't I seen you before?' she asked.

'I used to work in ante-natal about two years ago,' I replied, to which she responded, 'Well, what the devil are you doing here?'

I was mightily embarrassed to have been sprung, and instead of telling her my story, I just shrugged. The job I was doing was so dirty, wet, tedious and seemingly endless—pots and pans from staff and patients' overnight meals were piled up waiting for me when I arrived and constantly replaced throughout the day—it left me quite dispirited.

Buddy, Jimmy, Brunie and their daughter, Naomi, were also in Brisbane. However, they didn't live close by so we did not spend much time together. It was a great shock to me, therefore, to hear on the radio that Buddy had shot and killed a man. I went to visit Brunie, to see if she needed help, and found her in the process of changing her name on all her documents so that she could not be identified and associated with the crime. The dead man had been a musician at a club where Brunie worked. He had driven her home after work and an argument had ensued between him and Buddy.

I went with Brunie once to visit Buddy in prison. He was no longer the person I had known, happy and care-free. He cried and begged both of us not to come again, he didn't want us to see him in such a wretched state. The rifle had broken in two during the course of the argument, he'd claimed, and when he picked it up and pointed the barrel, bullets had come out in rapid succession. Several shots had penetrated the man's body through the same hole, a feat even an expert marksman would have had trouble performing, and he felt sure that forensic science would prove the murder was an accident. He was deeply distressed by the loss of life, and concerned for the relatives of the victim.

News of the case reached the north and again Mum wrote to me. 'Do all your friends commit murder? What is it about you that attracts these unsavoury types?' I was lost for an answer. I would have thought that apparently good, God-fearing church-goers were beyond involvement in any sort of crime. Brunie told me that because of the murder the Mormon Church would no longer accept their participation. I wondered also whether Buddy's involvement in this catastrophe meant that, under his Church's principles, in his next life he would come back black.

Dessie Mills, who by this time had left her alcoholic and abusive husband, Reg, was also living in Brisbane. She had picked up with a new partner, Pete, and she was running a fish shop and organising to open a book exchange. William and I agreed to take over the fish shop. Dessie had told us the hours were long but the rewards matched the effort put in and, inexperienced in business, we took her word for it. William continued to work outside and I ran the shop throughout the day while caring for Russel, and when William came home in the evening we shared the responsibility. It did not take us long to realise we were working day and night and still going downhill. No wonder Dessie had been so keen to palm the business off on to us, we thought. She was locked into a lease which, fortunately, she had not signed over to us. So we told her we were not prepared to continue.

Dessie didn't appear unduly upset by our decision, although she and her own children were then obliged to move back to the quarters behind the shop where we had been living. This was not long after Christmas, 1965. William and I had bought Russel a splendid pedal car, a big bright red fire engine complete with a little ladder. We had decided to move to Sydney, which seemed to offer better prospects, and we asked Dessie to look after our things until we could arrange for their transport when we found a place to live. We took our clothes but left all the worldly goods—sheets, towels and kitchenware—that we had accumulated, including Russel's fire engine.

William's and my life together had been punctuated by times of stress, brought about mainly through contact with people associated with me, such as Arthur and Dessie. So I reasoned that we might have a better chance starting again somewhere new. Intermittently I had been in touch by letter with Skip, who had struck up a relationship with another woman. They now had a child, and he wanted a divorce. I drove to Gatton, outside Brisbane, through a fierce storm to accommodate his wish to have divorce papers served on me. As I was with William, it seemed that a divorce would be in all our interests.

William had been talking for a while about his wish to go back to England to visit his mother. So, we were only in Sydney a short time, in share accommodation in a tiny house off Pitt Street, Redfern, when he sold the car and used the funds to leave.

I moved into a flat in the St James apartment building in East Sydney with my youngest sister, Leonie. We were joined briefly in the same apartment building, though not in the same flat, by Dellie, who had changed her name to Della, married a man named John, who worked for an airline company, and had a young son, Craig.

Della had completed a stenographer, receptionist and bookkeeping course, but she was appalled by the racism she confronted when she applied for positions that matched her skills. As well, her relationship with her husband was tense. John seemed to me to be a strange and aloof person, given to secretive comings and goings at all hours of the day and night.

When Mum learned that I was struggling to hold down a job and care for Russel, she seized upon the opportunity to visit us all. She said she was pleased to get away from Arthur, and hoped he would find somebody else to keep him out of gaol in her absence and even to look after him permanently. She planned to stay for six months.

Leonie had been wanting to find a place on her own, and Mum's imminent arrival prompted her departure. She moved into a room in Kings Cross and went through what Mum described as her 'arty phase', living by drawing and making jewellery to sell in the street. I had heard Leonie, on several occasions, telling some Chinese friends of ours that she was part-Chinese, and later informing some Japanese friends that she was part-Japanese. When I asked her about this, she'd told me her reason was that if there was another war, with the Chinese or the Japanese, she wanted them to spare her. The idea seemed half-baked, but when I reflected upon it later I felt that her behaviour and the strange lifestyle she adopted around that time were probably symptomatic of her confusion about her identity.

Although Russel was considered too young to start school, I applied to enrol him at the Catholic School just across the street because he was already so advanced. He knew his numbers and alphabet and was able to read, though his favourite reading was the TV guide. The nuns sent us to an office in the city to have him undergo some tests, which he passed with flying colours, so they let him start.

I had written to Dessie asking her to send down the tea-chests with all my home-making equipment in them, along with Russel's fire engine, but they hadn't arrived. Mum wrote to her too, but neither of us received a reply. So the flat was very make-do. Leonie and I had decorated the room with empty liqueur bottles scrounged from Beppi's restaurant, which was just below our window, placing them all on a high narrow shelf which ran around the entire room. Mum thought they looked terrible and fretted that if any of the nuns from Russel's school came by, they would think we were alcoholics.

Mum's fear was almost realised when I called to pick Russel up one day, and a young nun asked if she could come to the flat to talk about his progress. I had no option but to agree, though I stopped Mum from removing the bottles. 'I'm sure she'll know they're just decoration,' I told her. 'She knows we couldn't afford such expensive grog.'

After learning that we were lapsed Catholics, the nun came often and we shared many conversations. I was curious about why a very beautiful woman with extraordinarily grace had joined the order. In turn, she was just as curious about the things that motivated me, and we formed a warm friendship. Although her order forbade her from taking food or even a drink of water at our place, she would often drop over unexpectedly and, if it was convenient, spend an hour or so. Although I had enjoyed the companionship and support of Sister Sebastian during my school days, I had come to regard nuns and their restricted lifestyle, which prevented them from being in touch with the real world, in a very negative manner. This young woman gave me cause to re-evaluate my thoughts, and even after we had both left Sydney we continued to correspond.

Mum, who had never during my lifetime had a real holiday, found it difficult to adjust once Russel started school. I came home from work one day to find her weeping. I realised that she would find it impossible to cope with being alone throughout the day, so I picked up the newspaper and, like a miracle, found a part-time job vacancy at a kindergarten just three or four streets away. Mum applied and was accepted to clean and keep the kindergarten in order for a few hours each morning. She regaled us with the story of her interview. Another applicant had been interviewed before her, she said, and when the other woman left, the interviewer had said confidentially to Mum, 'A lovely lady, but I couldn't let her have the job. She wouldn't have been able to keep up. She was sixty if she was a day.' As Mum was also well over sixty, she hoped the interviewer wasn't going to ask her age!

I had found a good job working as a hostess in the Polynesian Room at the American National Club in Macquarie Street, in the city. It was an exclusive club for the very wealthy, with a limited membership. People who wanted to join were put on a waiting list. When a member died, if the next applicant on the list was suitably refereed, they were offered the membership. Evening meals were served in one of several dining rooms on the floor below ours, but lunch was taken at a smorgasbord in the Polynesian Room. Almost all the staff in the Polynesian Room were, as a general rule, non-white. A couple of Asian guys ran the bar, and a Maori woman, Lillian, and I usually spent our shifts working on the floor. The setting up and food arrangement for the weekday lunches were overseen by a white woman named Karen.

The work was very easy after some of the jobs I'd held. We wore long light cotton frocks with large tropical flowers printed on them, and the barmen wore tropical shirts. When people arrived on our floor, Lillian and I had to greet them by their names. When women arrived alone to wait to be joined by their husband or friends, we sat and talked with them so they did not feel or look like they were alone. When their company arrived, we offered to summon a bar steward to attend to them, then made ourselves scarce. When they weren't busy the barmen taught us how to make and serve a wide range of cocktails, and we perfected our silver service dexterity, skills which would come in very handy later. Much of my time was spent doing crosswords or reading, which we were permitted to do as long we stood up and if there were no members or guests on the floor.

We were, I supposed, hired to be decorative, servile, quietly attentive and non-threatening. The room boasted a huge photograph of a Hawaiian Island on the back wall, and we added to the atmosphere. Guests often asked where we were from, hoping perhaps that we hailed from Polynesia. When I answered 'Townsville' they often responded, 'No, where are you *really* from.' If I persisted with my answer, some became angry and abusive. 'You can't be Aboriginal,' they'd tell me, 'you're far too bright and pretty.' I was deeply disturbed by this attitude, though I had a sneaking feeling it was meant to be a compliment. My ambivalence increased when I was requested by the management to be photographed in our glamorous uniform by a noted photographer, Ted Roberts. Only six copies of one particular print were to be made, I was told. One to be sold on each of four continents, one for the club and one for me. Ted Roberts was famous for his exclusive prints.

The manager of the club, a Swiss, proposed to me. We had had no dates, no personal relationship of any description, but he had become aware of my situation—a single mother struggling by myself. When Russel became ill, he had offered to collect all Russel's dirty laundry and take it to his own flat to wash. I thought this was kind as the shared laundry facilities in my block meant that I had to sit on the roof and watch that our clothes didn't disappear while they were drying. His offer to marry me and give Russel and me a home came as a complete surprise. Mum, however, was William's strong advocate in his absence, not that I was seriously entertaining the idea of marrying a complete stranger. There was a feeling of deja vu about the situation, which made me think that there were perhaps a lot of very lonely men in the world.

William spent his whole time in England pining to come back. He wrote constantly saying that, although he greatly valued the opportunity to visit his mother, his heart was with me and he wanted to return and get married. He was working and saving every penny for his fare.

We were married in the Wayside Chapel, Kings Cross, in July 1966. Mum had returned to Townsville by then, but Della and Leonie, with their respective husbands, attended. So too, strangely, did two people—a brother and sister—who just turned up at the church, saying they were related to me. I was very surprised, but in the hurly-burly of the wedding photos and moving our gathering onto the reception, they left and I have never seen them again. I have often wondered who these people were and what their relationship was to me.

I had made a friend, Christine Nieniewska, who helped prepare the food for the reception. Living not far away in a small flat in Rushcutters Bay with her daughter, Justine, Christine had been a wonderful friend to me during William's absence, helping take care of Russel. Although I regularly saw my sisters, Christine had been my confidante during this time.

Della, completely disillusioned with her prospects in Australia, was planning to go to New Zealand to try her luck there. I was apprehensive on her behalf and yet envious of her courage to strike out for the great unknown. She had no idea whether New Zealand would offer her the opportunity to use her skills, but from her experience here she knew that Australia would not.

William had found a job working on the Sydney Harbour Bridge, and he hated it. He joked about it, saying he was expected to scrub the whole bridge down with steel wool, but he was extremely dissatisfied. On the night after our wedding, he told me to be ready to give notice at work, that we were going back to Townsville so he could find a better job. 'I don't want my wife to work,' he said.

'But I've always worked. I *like* working, and you've never said anything before,' I replied, shocked by the suddenness of his remark and the vehemence behind it.

'We weren't married before, so I wasn't in the position to tell you what to do. But now I am.' I felt an ominous shudder pass over me.

We had no money to buy a car, so we travelled to Townsville by train. I had learned from Mum and Aunty Glad that Dessie Mills did not intend to surrender my tea-chests. So, on the way through Brisbane, anticipating trouble from her and her tattooed lover, I went to the police station nearest her shop and asked one of the officers to accompany me. The store was closed and Dessie refused to come out. The young policeman entered the premises and came back with one tea-chest. It contained a bent and battered old aluminium pot, one anodised lid from my own pretty set of saucepans which didn't fit the pot, and some grubby ragged sheets that definitely weren't mine. Dessie had told the officer that this was all I had left with her. He was terribly embarrassed but said there was nothing more he could do. Gone were all the things I had collected and with which I had hoped to start my married life, along with Russel's bright red fire engine.

Okay, I thought, so Dessie has stolen these things. There's a lesson in this for me; I will harden my heart against her, and never speak to her again. At the same time, I was sad about having to make this resolution for my own emotional protection. I felt that I was losing many of the people with whom I had grown up. Leila, dead from suicide; Della, on her way to New Zealand, and I had had a premonition that it would be twenty years before she would return; and Leonie was heaven only knew where. At the time it felt as if I only really had Dessie left from my childhood group, and her betrayal was devastating.

When we arrived in Townsville, we found that tenants had recently vacated the cottage I had grown up in, and Mum said that if we would accommodate Nellie and William would do some work on the old timber house, which was in very poor shape, we could have it dirt cheap. William was an excellent handyman and amateur carpenter, ready to turn his hand to almost anything, so he jumped at the opportunity.

Taking an almighty chance that the years had wrought some attitudinal changes amongst the nuns at Saint Joseph's and Saint Patrick's, the school from which I had been expelled, I made an appointment to discuss enrolling Russel. The young nun with whom I had formed a friendship in Sydney had given me the idea that I should at least try.

I was not surprised to be interviewed by a nun who had been at the school during the time I had attended, but I was unprepared when she told me that she had no idea that I had been expelled. She was regretful, she said, that this had happened and would try to find out something about it. Russel had a glowing report from the Sydney convent, so she saw no reason why he could be refused now, except that he had not been baptised.

'I'll think about it,' I informed her. 'And I'll pray for you while you do,' she told me with a smile. 'Meanwhile I'll expect to see him next Monday. He can continue his Christian education while you think too.'

4

Townsville was in the process of rapid change. Australia was caught up in the Vietnam War and the Army had built a new barracks on the edge of town. Townsville had become the first and last stop for Army personnel on their way to the war. Nineteen-year-old men were leaving, they thought, to die, and for many it was the first time they were away from parental authority. They wanted to ensure that they were not going to die without having tasted the 'pleasures' of life. Hard drinking and roughly pursuing women of any age, they made the townspeople feel decidedly unsafe. Returning soldiers, too, brought in vices. Townsville was the first place in Australia outside of a capital city to have a drug clinic, and the clinic was on the base.

This small country town, where everyone knew almost everyone else, at least by sight, had been thrust into a new role by the influx. Bigger stores opened, rock'n'roll bands and stars added Townsville to their tour schedules. New movie theatres, hotels and nightclubs opened while the old ones received face-lifts.

On an expanse of vacant bushland out near Mum's

house in Aitkenvale, where she had moved to provide me with isolation during my pregnancy with Russel, the University College of Townsville was being built. It would cater for the growing educational needs of the area and was also attracting new people to Townsville. This was the first tertiary institution in north Australia and it promised to provide a focus for studies that related directly to life and rural pursuits in the tropics as well as to marine life in tropical waters.

William got a job with the council, painting white lines down the centre of roads. Many Murri families had moved into town. The tenants in old Mrs Sullivan's house, which Mum still owned, were a young Black family—Cedric Geia, his wife and baby. Cedric also worked for the council and as soon as we were settled and had purchased a car, Cedric and William drove to work together. Actually, since William had spent all his savings on his ticket back to Australia, I bought our first car, a fact which was later to become a bone of contention.

When he wasn't at work, William applied himself diligently to the task of renovating the house. Mum was happy to supply the timber, paint and whatever else was required. In no time at all, the run-down old house had built-in cabinets in the kitchen, bright paint and new floor coverings throughout. I sewed curtains, and between us we transformed the place into a home.

I learned to cook, particularly William's favourite meals. It took some adjusting for him to eat cold meats and salads in December. He missed the snow around this season, too, although one year we had a hail storm in the middle of summer which left the town temporarily strewn with white balls of ice. This was the nearest he came to satisfying his nostalgia.

Russel enjoyed school and quickly made friends. A sprinkling of other Black children now attended the Catholic school, unlike during my days there.

I felt enormously relieved when William said he would legally adopt Russel. He made the application and, surprisingly, we were visited by the police. Although natural children can arrive into virtually any circumstances, and children living with parents in defacto arrangements are not automatically called into question, the families of children who are being adopted are subjected to rigorous inspection.

By this time there were policewomen in Queensland, and it was a policewoman who came to our house. She had obviously read old police reports about the circumstances in which I had become pregnant with Russel. Consequently, her attitude towards William in his willingness to undertake the role of father and the nice home he appeared to be providing for us was almost congratulatory. William preened.

Our marriage and the subsequent adoption procedure gave me a tremendous feeling of security. I was able to obtain a new birth certificate for Russel on which William appeared as his father, even though William had not yet arrived in Australia at the time of Russel's birth. I recalled the trauma I had experienced when Mum had forced me to sign the papers regarding his birth, how I had squirmed to write 'unknown' in the box for 'Father', knowing the stigma this would bring Russel. Now, while he was still too young to appreciate the implications, Russel was given a new surname and the legitimacy that I had craved for him.

William and I had many good times together and with Russel. Initially William enjoyed what he thought of as my eccentricities, especially my relationship with

snakes. On a visit to Cairns once, we called on a man who kept a backyard zoo. When we saw two huge rock pythons in a large pen, I wanted to film them with William's little Super-8 home-movie camera. They were eighteen and twenty-feet long, and their girth was as thick as a big man's forearm. William's gallantry was such that he insisted on going into the cage and taking the film himself. I was very impressed with his courage, even when we got home and discovered his nervousness had caused the hand-held camera to shake wildly throughout the process, making the snakes all but indiscernible.

William liked to dance, too, but when we met he was not very good at it. Under my tutelage, though, he became quite proficient, and we developed a range of moves and techniques that often caused other dancers to clear the floor just to watch us. With my Polynesian friend, Ena, we chased music and dance venues all over town and rarely missed an opportunity to attend a party,

as long as it involved dancing. Ena and I spent hours getting ready for these events, and for a giggle I'd often wear
a blond wig, very much in vogue at the time. Thus attired,
we attended parties—one at which Johnny O'Keefe was a
guest—and we always had a very good time.

William began to yearn for a child, as he said, 'of his
own'. He encouraged Russel, who was just beginning to
comment that all his friends had brothers and sisters,
and between them they put a great deal of pressure on
me. I wondered why I had not become pregnant and
went to the hospital to find out if there was a physical
reason for my apparent sterility. There I met a young
doctor, Alan Saltau, who, with his wife Jan, were to
become part of our growing circle of new friends.

Alan recommended a procedure wherein, under a
general anaesthetic, a light gas is blown through the
fallopian tubes to remove any blockages. This operation is not difficult, but it is painful for a week or so.
However, it seemed a small sacrifice to make in order
for us to become a thoroughly blood-related family.

The operation was successful and soon I had con-
ceived. Unlike my earlier pregnancies, this was a time
of joy for me, despite morning sickness, afternoon and
evening sickness, and nausea from the smell of just
about everything throughout the entire period. Jan
Saltau came by the house frequently and gorged herself
on mangoes from our trees. She, too, was pregnant and
craved this fruit.

Around this time I became concerned about William's
relationship with Cedric. Feeling nauseated, I often
stayed in bed as late as possible before taking Russel to
school. Each morning I could hear William call to Cedric,
letting him know that he was about to leave and if Cedric
wanted a lift, he was to come now. William's tone of

voice, over time, began to sound very nasty. There was a bullying, bossy element in it that either I had not noticed before or which was entirely new.

One night I cautioned William about his tone of voice, but he pooh-poohed me. The next evening he told me that he had asked Cedric if he found his manner offensive, and Cedric had said no. But a few days later, William came home from work with his head bandaged. At first he refused to tell me what had happened. Then he said he had given Cedric an order at work, and that Cedric had hit him with a piece of timber. We were not to discuss it further, he said, but I noticed that he was not giving Cedric a lift any more, and I heard that Cedric had been moved off William's road-marking gang.

I began to worry, not just about William and Cedric's relationship, but about a pattern of behaviour of white workers towards their black co-workers that had always deeply concerned me. Racism has many faces. William's unconsciously offensive manner towards Cedric was one of them.

William was also often short with other Murri friends who came to visit me, and with children from another branch of the large Geia clan who lived two doors away on the corner of Hale and Stanley streets.

One day, early on in our marriage, I had been turning the mattress over when I found a letter hidden there. It was in William's mother's handwriting and the envelope was open. From time to time, William had shared his mother's letters with me, so I had no qualms about reading it. The letter contained only ordinary family news, which made me wonder why William had concealed it, until I came to a paragraph in which his mother wrote that he was lucky not to be in England now as the country was changing for the worse. 'Black-ies,' she wrote, were even working in stores in her area and the whole place was going to pot.

When William came home I asked him if he had told his mother that I was coloured. 'No,' he replied, 'she wouldn't understand.'

'What will you do when our baby arrives?' I asked.

'I'll worry about that when the time comes,' he told me.

I was concerned and hurt that William continued to conceal from his relations the true nature of our inter-racial marriage. He hadn't sent wedding photos to his mother or his sister, and although he had informed them that we were expecting a child, and they subsequently sent parcels of wonderful baby clothes, I somehow felt that we were living a lie.

By this time I had many friends around Townsville. Some were new to the town, others, usually older than me, had known me as a child but now welcomed me as an adult. Mrs Lucy Mitchell was one such person; she lived three doors away from us. Mrs Mitchell was active in theatre productions, and she sought me out and tried to involve me. We discussed the absence of Murris on television and, with her encouragement, I wrote to Crawford Productions in Melbourne and put to them some blunt questions about why this was so. I received a letter which explained that they accepted appli-cations from anyone, and if I or my friends wanted to apply, we were to fill out forms (enclosed) and send voice tapes and photographs of ourselves. I hastily rounded up a small group of young Blacks, and we filled in the forms. Mrs Mitchell coached us and assisted us to prepare the voice tapes.

Despite the effort and expense we went to in order

to fulfil Crawford Production's requirements, we heard nothing more and, with time, became very disappointed. This was in 1963 and we didn't realise then that we were more than thirty years too early. Even at the time of writing this book, the appearance of Blacks in ordinary support roles, such as a waitress or taxi-driver, in Australian films is still in the future. Black actors have occasional cameo roles but are not seen as part of the everyday fabric of Australian society in movies or television productions.

I became friends with Henry and Margaret Reynolds, who were comparatively new to the town. Margaret, a specialist teacher for the deaf, and Henry, a historian, had come up from Tasmania. Although they had had little or no opportunity to meet and interact with Black people previously, they were unpleasantly surprised by the blatant discrimination against Blacks which they now observed.

A handful of Blacks in Townsville were already active in pushing for change, amongst them Evelyn Scott and my old friend Eddie (Koiki) Mabo. Evelyn was involved with the Federal Council for the Advancement of Aboriginal and Torres Strait Islanders (FCAATSI), but she made time, despite also raising her large family, to attend meetings of the One People of Australia League (OPAL). Both these organisations were based in the south, but local meetings were enthusiastic and spirited.

It was into this environment and circle of friends that I gave birth to my daughter, Naomi. Margaret Reynolds loaned me an English pram and a few other items of baby furniture. I had had very little for Russel when he was born, he'd grown up in my arms because I could not afford a pram, so I was very pleased to have the relief of not always carrying the baby. Margaret and Henry's own children were young too, and we swapped items between us as needs arose or as our children grew out of them.

Margaret had an aura of sophistication about her which I found very attractive. She spoke her mind on any issue and let the chips fall wherever. She wasn't just talk, either. The movement for sexual desegregation of hotel bars had reached Townsville, with women going into bars and chaining themselves to bar-rails when they weren't served. Until then, women had been restricted to meeting and drinking in small back rooms, known as ladies' lounges. If husbands and wives went out together, they could both sit in the ladies' lounge, although few men chose to do so, probably for fear of ridicule from their drinking mates. Women, however, were forbidden to enter men's bars, and women who worked in these bars were often regarded quite negatively. Margaret had been active in this movement and seemed to me to be extremely well versed in women's liberation philosophy. Her friendship stirred my thoughts and she made me feel that it was alright to voice my concerns and ideas.

Russel was delighted to have a sister, and delighted, in this instance, is very much an understatement. He really regarded Naomi as his own, and assumed a fair measure of responsibility for her. Naomi was a highly excitable child, so much so that it caused many problems. She would start chuckling to herself and bring up her food. As I began to wean her, I found I had to prepare twice the amount of vegetable puree each time in order to have the second serve on hand for after she'd brought up the first one. I fed her in a darkened room to minimise the possibility of distraction. One day a beautiful butterfly alighted on the window pane while Naomi was eating. She immediately noticed it and worked her tiny self up into a frenzy, rocking backwards and forwards in her high-chair until, of course, she brought up her whole meal. Doctors told me to keep her sedated, but I opposed the idea of a quick fix involving medication.

Russel took Naomi out almost daily, walking her around the neighbourhood in a stroller. He'd call to neighbours to come and look at her. 'Hasn't she grown since yesterday?' he often asked them. He hovered about her constantly, casting over her an enduring mantle of love and protection.

William left the council to try his hand at setting up his own painting contracting business. It was hard at first; most home and business-owners in Townsville were 'old blood' with established ways of getting things done. They traded contracts for work amongst themselves and generally knew each by first name. William was very much 'a newcomer'.

Mum, although she did move in the social circles of the 'old blood', had been in the town for decades and had built up a reputation as reliable, hard working and trustworthy. She owned property and had used the services of the same bank ever since I was a child. She spoke to the manager of this bank, telling him that William had married her daughter. Consequently, William's first significant contract was to paint the bank, which was located in the middle of the main street. Shopkeepers and other bank customers saw him at work, and his business built up from the exposure.

However, in the slow days as he was trying to get established, money was very tight for us. He suggested

I look for work, which surprised me as he had made such a fuss about this in Sydney.

Lowth's Hotel, on the corner of Stanley and Flinders streets, was undergoing a major refurbishment. In its previous life, it had been very dowdy. Mum's old friend Nellie had worked there as cook. As children, we'd peer through the small window almost at kerb level into the dark kitchen where she plied her skills, and when she saw us she would come out and give us treats. The refurbishment included the erection of a tower of rooms and a very swish foyer, which soon became the talk of the town.

One morning I read an advertisement in the *Townsville Daily Bulletin*, calling for staff for the Lowth's dining room and cocktail bar. Although I had worked in salubrious surroundings in Sydney, they had been, I thought, exotic-specific, and I was not sure whether Townsville was ready to see a Black woman working in a similar role. Many hotels around town didn't serve or admit Blacks, and the referendum that would begin to change this was still some years away.

Response to the advertisement may have been slow because when I rang from a nearby public phone after midday, the woman who answered sounded desperate.

'I'm ringing about the positions advertised in this morning's paper. Do you hire coloured people?' I was quick to ask, wishing to save myself embarrassment. I had chosen to phone instead of going into the hotel, even though we lived only three blocks from it, so that, if the answer was no, the person on the other end of the phone would never have the satisfaction of knowing who she had refused. I also didn't want to waste her time or my own by discussing details only to find at the end of the conversation that the position wasn't open to me.

'I hire anyone who can work! Can you work?'

'I'll be in to see you in thirty minutes,' I replied.

Mrs Kendricks, the manager, was frazzled when I arrived but sat down and concentrated on talking with me. I explained that I was interested in the cocktail bar position and that I had learned to make cocktails at the American National Club. She was impressed, but she explained that the cocktail bar wouldn't be finished for two weeks. In the meantime, she asked if I would like to work the liquor outlet in the main dining room.

I had pictured myself finely dressed in a black skirt and lacy white blouse, shaking frothy drinks into sugar-rimmed glasses, but I agreed to take the other position until the cocktail bar opened. I was to start immediately in the Peacock Room, even though there was minor work still to be completed in that section too. The hotel management wanted to open for business as quickly as possible to recoup some of the enormous outlay spent on the redevelopment.

When I arrived for work that evening, Mrs Kendricks took me aside. I feared she may have had a change of mind, and I was ready to bolt when she spoke.

She had had trouble finding trained waitresses, she told me, and wanted to know whether I knew how to wait on tables and if I had silver service experience. A look of relief came over her face when I said yes, but I saw the much lighter job of opening and serving wines going down the drain. Would I, as a big favour to her, help her in the dining room that night, she asked. One of the men from the downstairs bar could handle the wines, but the dining room couldn't function with the few untrained staff she had so far assembled.

Mrs Kendricks and one other woman and I served the dining room that night. I was surprised to see Mrs Kendricks running backwards and forwards with orders and plates, darting up to the check-out desk as people departed, and running up and down the stairs to other sections of the hotel to try to keep the whole place operating. Her workload was so great that I felt sorry for her.

She, however, was very impressed with my work. I had demonstrated my ability to step in behind her and take over during her absences, keeping orders and meals flowing and ensuring customers were not uncomfortably aware of the staff shortage. The chefs were top workers too, and very cooperative once they saw that I knew what I was doing. The dining room had been well patronised that night as the townsfolk were curious to see the flash new interior and be amongst the first to be able to talk about the quality of the place.

When the night's work was over, Mrs Kendricks voiced her appreciation and asked if I would take over training dining-room staff. She had received applicants, she said, who were keen but didn't have a clue about the work, hadn't even heard of silver service. She also said she wanted the dining-room staff to wear distinctive uniforms, not just black skirts and white shirts, and would value my input into this. That night I went home tired but happy with my acceptance.

The uniform, when it was designed, consisted of slacks and a long sleeveless vest which came down well over the top of the pants and buttoned right up to the neck. We chose an orange cotton print, which was very flattering on me and stood out well against the more sombre colours of the dining-room walls and furniture.

Much later, variations in the uniform's colours were introduced as it became obvious that the first choice, although very smart, didn't suit everybody.

William was pleased with the boost in our income and agreed to look after the children at night. He would arrive home at around five in the evening, and I'd feed the children, prepare his meal, then leave for work. As I was also responsible for the children during the day, getting Russel to and from school and taking care of the shopping and housework, and my work at the hotel often didn't finish until well after midnight, it was a long day. It was fortunate that I worked so close to where we lived.

Once William's business picked up, however, he began to nag me to leave the hotel. Responsibility for the children had always fallen on me, and when it was necessary for him to care for them for a few hours, he did so not as a parent but as a favour to me. Now he begrudged looking after the children five nights a week and felt this impinged on his freedom. He sought to recruit Mum to plead his case for him. Mum came by and told me confidentially that she didn't agree with him, that she was aware he had welcomed the injection of money into his business when he needed it, and that his reasons for wanting me to stop working were selfish. She said she thought he resented me getting dressed up in my smart uniform every night and going off without him. If I had a job where I worked in a dowdy dress and with a bucket and mop, he would probably be quite happy. He was just using the children as an excuse.

'Eventually you'll have to make a choice,' she said, 'because he isn't going to let up. It will come down in the end to your marriage or your job. You have to think about that, about which one you want most.'

When I told Mrs Kendricks that I would have to leave, she pleaded with me to stay on in some capacity. Would I take over service in the function room? The work was irregular, only when there were bookings for wedding parties and the like, which wouldn't create the same strain at home.

I agreed. I welcomed the opportunity to mix with people outside the house, people I wouldn't ordinarily have met in my role as housewife and mother. I was also very good at my job, able to walk into the dining room and spot a salt shaker missing on a table, a spoon not quite straight, a serviette not properly folded. I knew which foods were served on which plates, what cutlery was required for any course, indeed everything there was to know about the smooth operation of a large-scale, first-class hotel dining facility. At functions it was my job to allocate service areas to staff, oversee the efficient delivery of meals and the removal of plates and tablepieces afterwards, and my personal task was to wait on the head table, which was always where bridal parties were seated. The job brought me a respect that I didn't receive very much elsewhere, as shop assistants often left me waiting until they had served all the white customers, for example.

William was not happy even with this more limited involvement in the hotel. He said if I was going to continue to work, it had to be for the benefit of the family, not for my personal satisfaction. In that case, I had to carry all the expenses of the house and he would use his income to expand the painting business. As I was a partner in the business, he said, this would be to my own advantage in the long term. I didn't think this was very fair, though, because I never seemed to have a cent to spend on anything I wanted. My money went on food and the domestic bills.

Over time, William found a great deal to criticise about me. He complained that I was 'fanatical' about anything I took up, that everything had to be perfect to please me. When my activities benefited him, such as when I sewed almost all our clothes, including his work clothes, he said he appreciated all the money we saved. When I pursued educational ends, however, he raised objections. He particularly resented the time I spent reading, even when I was reading child psychology books about how best to bring up our children.

William also, in the main, did not like my friends. He said he had nothing in common with Margaret and Henry Reynolds, and refused the occasional invitations to their home for a meal. Consequently, Margaret and I shared mainly lunches, something I did not regret. I enjoyed hearing her perspective on a range of political issues. We sometimes met in the Lowth's Hotel lower bar for lunch. One of my warmest memories of that period of my friendship with Margaret is of the day when, after months of drinking orange juice, I succumbed and took a vodka and orange at midday with my meal. To me this was the epitome of waywardness. That afternoon I pushed the pram with baby Naomi sleeping in it up the hill to my house, a little light-headed and feeling deliciously rebellious.

My main complaint about William was his possessiveness, which surfaced in a multitude of ways. He seemed to feel that he 'owned' me and resented any time that I spent doing anything that he could not relate directly to himself. He sometimes burned my books if I read them instead of watching television programs alongside him. He became jealous of anyone I spoke to, including women, and he would make nasty remarks about them within their earshot.

As well, his attitude towards my Murri friends was far from desirable, though I have since realised that his attitude is shared by many white people. Generally he did not object if I helped them, but he did not like me socialising with them. Indeed, he was quite tolerant of anyone I brought to the house in need of assistance, and there were many, but he did not like to come home and find a group of us sitting around having a cup of tea and a yarn.

Thinking about this over time, I came to believe that William felt that my marriage to him, a white person, elevated me. I was expected to assume the role of advocate and patron, a position with which he obviously felt comfortable. It didn't seem to occur to him that my Murri friends were *my* support network, that we talked about the racism we suffered and ways to overcome it.

Mum could see that I was again becoming increasingly unhappy with my life and that I felt I was stagnating. She offered to pay for a correspondence course to enable me to do Senior, the Queensland equivalent of university entrance. I was cheered by this, and enthusiastic. The only subject I couldn't manage alone was French, but the Technical College held evening classes. William resented my attendance at these classes, and when he discovered that the teacher was a man, he burned all my French books and forbade me to go. Within a few months I abandoned the course altogether because of his attitude.

Meanwhile, I had been busy attending as many meetings as possible of the local chapter of OPAL. We had participated in a demonstration against McKim-

mins, a Flinders Street store which had never hired anyone of colour. Flowing from the demonstration, we were invited to put up a display of Aboriginal cultural artefacts. Koiki Mabo and I did most of the work collecting the pieces. On the day Koiki turned up with coconut fronds which he plaited right there in the store to make mats on which we stood the items.

Members began to ask me to represent OPAL, although the organisation was multi-racial and there were more qualified members than me. I was sent as the local delegate to attend regional and state meetings, first to Cairns and later to Brisbane. I was also invited to give presentations about OPAL and our goals to local service clubs. When William was unwilling to look after the children, my friends quite happily took over the task.

A small group of us planned to attend the Cairns regional meeting, and to travel there by bus. On the day, I was waiting at the bus depot when I had a feeling that I should go home and catch a later bus. Without really knowing why, I did so, and was upset to learn that the bus I had forgone had been involved in an accident. No one was seriously injured, but I wished I had been surer about my premonition so that I could at least have alerted the passengers.

The Brisbane conference was extremely educational for me. The series of speakers opened my mind to the possibility of creating opportunities for people of colour which had hitherto not existed. I met John New-fong, who would later become an active player in the Black movement in the south.

Throughout this period, the peaceful activism we were involved in unfortunately drew the attention of authorities. Our phones were tapped. Margaret Reynolds' house was broken into, and stolen papers were later returned by police who claimed to have found them in Flinders Street. One of the letters still had a pound note attached to it, which was a donation towards the struggle, so the police story seemed highly unlikely.

Through Mrs Mitchell I had met a man who had been a television news cameraman in the south, but had become disillusioned with the callousness he found in the industry. He still had an Arriflex camera and wanted to help us. With his assistance, at a FCAATSI conference held in Townsville, I interviewed some very courageous Aboriginal people, including Vincent Lingiari, the Gurindji Elder who led his people on a strike against appalling work conditions. We were disturbed when the film disappeared on its way back from processing in the south, something that had never happened to this man's work in the past.

Major problems arose during the organisation of the conference, too. Evelyn Scott had booked the former migrant hostel, which was now being hired out to groups, for delegates to stay in. But almost on the eve of the event she was informed that it was 'unavailable'. Palm Island delegates were enormously disadvantaged when they learned that the two boats which regularly serviced the island were to be put up on slips for repair. For both boats to be out of commission simultaneously was unprecedented.

Driving home early one afternoon from the conference, I was curious to see a van parked in front of an empty scout hall on an otherwise long deserted stretch of road close by the conference venue. I did a U-turn and pulled up behind it. I was startled when the back door of the van opened and a man hopped out. Behind him I could see that the van was fitted out with recording equipment. The man stood blinking for a moment while his eyes adjusted to the bright sunlight, and when he was able to make out my car, he took fright and jumped straight back into the van. I returned to the conference and told organisers what I'd seen. They laughed—it was a public meeting, anyone could have come and recorded the sessions. It didn't make any sense at all that the powers-that-be should choose to record the conference covertly from a van parked out in the tropical heat.

The fact that we were under surveillance by ASIO became something of a laughing matter. Hearing any interference or static on our phone lines we would often joke, and ask, 'Are you hearing us loud and clear, ASIO?'

Margaret Reynolds invited me to a ladies' luncheon being held at a seaside hotel at which the renowned Faith Bandler was to speak. I had never been to anything like this and amused Margaret by fretting about what I should wear. As I suspected, I was the only woman of colour there, apart from Faith. Although I turned up nicely decked out for the day, Faith's appearance blew me away and still remains in my mind. She was the *most* elegant woman I had ever seen, beautifully groomed and wearing absolutely spotless little white gloves. It was unusual to see anyone wearing gloves in North Queensland's tropical heat, and the difficulty involved in keeping them so pristine was a feat in itself. When I saw how this room full of white women responded so positively to the manner in which Faith presented herself, her calm way of explaining the ramifications of the upcoming referendum, what it would mean to race relations and how voters should seize this opportunity for change, I was completely entranced.

I was becoming increasingly active in the struggle. The ABC invited me to give a radio interview with the journalist Jim Downes. Afterwards he asked if I'd join him at a nearby hotel for a drink and a chat about the program. We had just settled down when a female attendant came and told Jim, 'We'll serve you but we won't serve her. Hotel policy.' Jim was staggered. He had just completed an interview with me in which he had implied that the energies we at OPAL were putting into calling for change were not really warranted.

Much later I flew to Sydney to spend a week with a friend, Carol Neist. I took the opportunity to visit the Foundation of Aboriginal Affairs, as I had heard many positive things about it. Mr Tom Williams met me and showed me around the Foundation's offices. He then took me to lunch, and he discussed the goals of the Foundation, its history and operations, and I gave him an update on issues we were confronting in North Queensland. We were both delighted at the result of the recent referendum held in May 1967, which had, we thought, admitted Aboriginal people into full citizenship, but we were disappointed by the lack of action flowing from it. We began to wonder what it meant.

On my return to Townsville, Tom Williams wrote a couple of letters to me. When William discovered them he became very angry and said he suspected me of having had an affair with Tom. Nothing could have been further from the truth. Tom, an older man, had impressed me with his quiet manner and the determination and commitment which shone through in his voice. I had dropped in unannounced and found that he wore a suit at the office, something I had not seen before but which I felt set a very positive standard and provided local youth with an excellent role model for achieving success. But apart from these impressions and their political impact, I knew virtually nothing about the man and said so to William.

By this time we had installed a phone at the house, which William needed to run his business. One day some people I didn't know rang and asked if I could come and see them urgently. At the small market garden which they ran, they told me that they employed a Torres Strait Islander who also lived in a tiny shack on their property. He had been arrested, they felt wrongfully, but they had no one they could turn to for help. They had seen me interviewed on television and found my name in the phone book.

I had previously been called on to do odd jobs that no one else knew how to handle. A young destitute Black woman of limited intellectual ability had been found being abused by men in the street. I'd taken her home and given her a roof, meals, and even some responsibility around the place, until she got back on her feet. She had eventually married a white man who also lacked a full intellectual capacity and, to everyone's surprise, they had a child who they doted on much more lovingly and carefully than many parents with far fewer handicaps.

The case of the arrested gardener was a new problem for me, and initially I didn't have a clue how to handle it. By then I had an extensive network, and outside my direct circle of contacts were people I had gone to school with, some of whom had become professionals around the town. Although they hadn't put their hands up to help, I felt that they could, in an emergency, be imposed upon.

The police alleged that the gardener had stolen a gold watch. The gardener, who had a very poor command of English and also limited intellectual ability, told us that he and a woman companion had been beaten up by a number of white men and gone to Casualty for treatment. When the police were called to the hospital, one of them had produced a gold watch from the gardener's clothes, which were on the floor because he was wearing a hospital smock while his injuries were being attended to. He was sure the watch had not been in his possession prior to their arrival.

When at last the case came before the court, the gardener had legal representation. The judge heard the man's difficulty with speech and realised that the gardener was unable to tell the time, and that his lifestyle did not require him to do so. Why, then, would he have stolen a watch? The judge dismissed the case against him.

There were no Aboriginal legal services at this time. It would be almost a decade before the concept was developed and formally acted upon by the Townsville Black community.

Although I had chosen to stay away from the court during the hearing, the police may have learned of my involvement through their discussions with the market garden proprietors. The information was innocent enough but from then on, often when I was out on the street alone, the police would stop me. This was especially the case after I finished work late at night at Lowth's Hotel. Although we lived only three blocks away, the presence of the Army recruits had made the streets unsafe for women alone after dark, so I always travelled by car. Sometimes the same policemen from the previous night would be waiting beside my car when I came out, and they would again ask me for my licence and registration papers, and carry out a full-scale inspection of the vehicle at that late hour. Once when they found a tyre and rim off William's work truck in the boot waiting to be repaired, the police threatened to book me for having a bald spare tyre. They only backed off when I pointed out how much larger that tyre was than the tyres on my car.

A number of times men followed me home after work. They didn't know me from Adam, hadn't spoken to me, but, on seeing a Black woman driving alone, they did foolish and dangerous things such as tailgating my car, and flashing their lights at me from behind. As we lived in a cul de sac, once these strangers pulled into our little laneway behind me there was nowhere they could easily go. On occasions William had to come bursting out of our house and chase them away. Once, he followed a car back into town where it reached high speeds along the main streets, but he managed to get its number before it disappeared from view. When he saw the car again a few days later, he followed it to the top of Castle Hill before approaching the driver, whose wife was sitting beside him. The driver told William that he had been on duty at the Army base on the night of the incident, but had loaned his car to friends who he was reluctant to name. His wife was extremely unamused.

At other times, when I was walking in the street, I was approached by strange men who propositioned me. Some of these creatures were both ugly and dirty. They would indicate that they had a bottle of beer in the brown paper bag under their arm, and in return for my sexual favours they would offer me half. Unfortunately these incidents happened frequently, and deeply distressed me. I would often flee in alarm and suffer nightmares and flashbacks for days. I resented the fact that these men obviously thought my value was half a bottle of beer. I was unable to report any of this to the police, because the police were now lined up in my mind with the harassers.

I became increasingly withdrawn from William. Although he didn't condone these emotional assaults, he felt that they were petty and that, if anything serious happened, I should turn to him for protection. He couldn't see that there was a whole system of racism at work which produced these events. Indeed, this system even encouraged them by maintaining Blacks in a position of vulnerability and at the bottom of all the totem poles, economically and socially. This system had to be overturned.

The more I withdrew, the more angry and desperate William became to hang on to me and restrict my freedom. He would come home from work, change and go out again, leaving me with no one to care for the children on nights when I had to go to work. Sometimes I could arrange a sitter from amongst women who also worked at the hotel who I knew were not rostered on that night, but at other times I had to ring in and cancel.

I was also unhappy about the manner William had begun to adopt towards Russel. I objected to the apparently careless blows he sometimes landed on the child; Russel seemed to be ducking a lot. William regularly went out to the Barrier Reef on fishing expeditions with his friends, and I had to beg him on a few occasions to take Russel along. More ominously, though, he derided Russel because he loved to dance. After one such incident, Russel had come to me in tears and asked, 'Mum, what's a poofter?' He suffered no scars or bruises, but I worried about the emotional damage.

William had also begun raising his voice and threatening to hit me. Late one night, after I had just come home from work, William held me against a wall and threw a punch which landed close to my head, narrowly missing my face. He said that the next time his punch would land on me. This blow was so hard that he fractured his hand and had to have it set and put in a splint for six weeks. I knew then that our marriage was over; I was not prepared to live in constant fear. I told him that I wouldn't leave him while he was handicapped and unable to carry on his business, but I planned to use the six weeks to arrange my affairs so that I could leave.

Those weeks seemed interminable. I was kept buoyed, however, by dreams that I'd begun to have sometime ago and which continued during that period. Much earlier, disenchanted with the quality of many of the things I'd been reading, I'd taken to the typewriter and started to write my own stories and articles. Then a voice came into my dreams telling me that this was the direction in which I was to go. I should move to the south, said this man's voice, where I would become a journalist and author. I thought this voice belonged to my deceased father, whoever he might have been, and that he was directing me from beyond the grave, from a place where he could see not only the past but also the future.

I spoke to Margaret Reynolds and told her of this dream and my growing ambition. Margaret cautioned me, telling me that journalists have been to schools where they learned to do that type of work. I thought this may have been the case because I had noticed a certain sameness about many of the things I'd been reading. Nevertheless, I felt that, without the inhibitions imposed by learning all the rules, my writing would be exploratory and fresh. I might be a trendsetter rather than a follower. I had no idea of the risks that such a path would entail.

While William's hand was knitting, I was invited to Evelyn Scott's house for a meeting with Denis Walker. We had heard news of growing militancy in the south, that Kath Walker's son had started a National Tribal Council in Brisbane, and I was eager to learn more. Much earlier, Neville Bonner had come up from Brisbane and held a meeting with us in an effort to gain our support for his bid to be placed on the Liberal Senate ticket. People who had known him when he had been working as a Native Police officer on Palm Island had politicised the meeting by telling us how Bonner had behaved towards his fellow Murris while in that position. Our response to him was not as warm as it may otherwise have been, although he later won the place on the ticket and was elected to the Senate.

Denis had no such history in the north. When I first saw him, holding court on Evelyn's verandah, he was wearing a trim afro, a black suit and sporting gold chains around his neck and his wrist. He exuded charisma and carried himself with such pride that we were impressed. His sophisticated presentation had a clarity and relevance that excited us all, providing us with a much needed infusion of hope.

'We need all Blacks involved in the struggle,' he told us, 'people prepared to do whatever's necessary to force the system to recognise our equality and end discrimination.' I said that I was leaving Townsville to go south within a few weeks, and asked him where he thought I should go.

'Sydney's where the action will happen,' he said. 'There are many young Blacks working there and lots more support. It's closer to Canberra, we have to put pressure on federal politicians to honour the referendum. But come by the Tribal Council in Brisbane on your way. You'll be made very welcome.'

I had been worried about the major decision I was making to leave my marriage and my many Townsville friends. I had few friends elsewhere, and the idea of starting out anew scared me. Denis' words suggested a warm reception would be waiting in the south if I was prepared to throw my weight into the struggle for change. I had two small children for whom I wanted a better life and greater opportunities than had been possible for me. My decision to leave, I felt, was right.

5

Originally I had planned to drive to Sydney with my personal effects stored in the boot of the car. I'd bought a stereo that I was very fond of, and had a record and small book collection, which, although inexpensive, was valuable to me. But the history of the car was a problem. I had bought the first car we owned. It wasn't fancy but it got us around when we had no other way to travel, and Townsville is a difficult place to live without a car. When William became more financial, he traded my car in on one which he put in both our names. Then, without approval or consultation with me, he traded the second car in on another in his name only. I was angry that the mateship amongst men around used car lots was such that this could happen so easily. Women were still deemed to own nothing of their own, everything of economic value belonged to the men in the family. My car had somehow disappeared.

By the time of my decision to leave, William also owned a truck, so I drove the car most of the time. Our arguments about the ownership of it were never resolved, but I felt it was mine. Although William made the payments, he could only do so because I had carried the financial burden of everything else concerned with the house. As well, I was a partner in the painting business, and had never received one penny from my initial investment.

I used the car to drive Russel to Charters Towers where I had arranged for him to board for one term at the Catholic school. This, I thought, would give me time to establish myself in the south, and find a place where the children and I could live. It would give Russel the option of remaining at the school if he liked it and if I could afford it, or coming south to live with me.

William was ambivalent about my leaving. He'd try to sweet-talk me into changing my mind and when I held firm he would bang and kick the furniture. And he'd do both these things over a space of just a few minutes. Then he'd help me make my departure arrangements, thinking that if he behaved reasonably it would later weigh in his favour and I would return. However, he was unable to maintain a sense of reason over any length of time. As the day drew near for me to leave, he hid the car, put my clothes under lock and key, and I would have had to fight him to remove anything I owned from the house.

I had earlier sorted through my clothes and left a pile of things which were fairly worn out at a girlfriend's house to be given away to people who needed them. So, when William refused to let me take my good clothes, I asked my friend to put the old clothes in a suitcase and leave them for me at the railway station. These, and my sweet young daughter, Naomi, ended up being the sum total that I carried away with me from a relationship that had lasted seven years.

I reflected on this as the train raced through the night towards Brisbane, bearing my child and me towards our new life. I had promised to meet William three months hence, on neutral ground, to discuss our respective lives and whether there was any point in continuing our marriage. I knew deep down, however, that he was unlikely to be able to change to accommodate my needs, and I would never be the obedient wife he required in order to find happiness.

Aunty Glad welcomed us for a few days' stopover, and she looked after Naomi the night before I left while I went to the National Tribal Council headquarters. Denis sent a van to pick me up after I rang him. It was driven by Cheryl Buchanan, who would later become a staunch friend.

The headquarters consisted of a large open-plan office, and even though it was nightfall many people were still working and the place was a hive of activity. Denis and many of the others were folding papers and stuffing envelopes to be mailed, so I sat on the opposite side of his desk and joined in the task while we talked.

Playing around on the floor was a child who was, from time to time, getting into mischief. Denis, whose conversation was littered with swear-words, struck out with his foot, narrowly missing the little one. This was not the Denis I had seen in Townsville, where he had been very cool, respectful and polite. Quite early in our conversation as he was explaining the set-up and goals of the council, I leaned over and, smiling, said quietly to him, 'Denis, don't swear.'

Behind me I heard the room full of people turn still and silent. A tense moment passed, during which Denis was frowning and looking down, then he raised his head and replied, 'Okay. If it's important to you, okay.' I thought I'd stretch my luck so I added, 'And don't kick the child.' He hadn't actually kicked the child, but he knew what I meant. I'd taken objection to his feinting towards the lad as an effort to instil fear into him. 'Okay,' Denis said without hesitation, and the room regained its clatter.

Denis gave me names, an address and phone numbers of people he thought I should contact on my arrival in Sydney: Paul Coe, Gary Foley, Gary Williams, Sekia Holland, all unknown to me. He asked me to send him my address when I got settled, and to stay in touch. I agreed. Cheryl drove me home.

This meeting, brief though it was, proved to be a pivotal event for me. My ideas about joining forces with the Black movement and using my skills to write began to gain form. At last I could see that I had the means to make a worthwhile contribution. Someone was writing the copy for the brochures and pamphlets we had been stuffing in the envelopes, and with a bit of practice that could be me.

In Sydney, however, the enormity of my undertaking gradually became evident as I tried to become established and find a place to live. A friend, Margaret Hudson, who had also worked at Lowth's Hotel, invited me to stay with her at her small Kings Cross flat until I could find something more permanent.

Margaret was managing a Cahill's restaurant in an underground arcade in the city, and her long working day started before dawn and ended after dark. She allowed Naomi and me to sleep in her little dayroom and was tremendously encouraging in my search.

Naomi, however, was three years old, and had never been happy to travel. Unlike Russel, she seemed unable to get through a few minutes without demanding the total attention of another person. Also she had to be thoroughly familiar with the environment around her before she felt secure. We'd always had to carry her own plate, cup and eating utensils, as well as the odd items she clung to for a security blanket, whenever we'd travelled outside the house.

I had thought I would be able to find a place for her in a play school, as she had been attending one in Townsville, but this proved to be impossible. I was told that, even as a single parent, I'd have to be working for her to qualify. I explained that if Naomi could be in care, I *would* be working, but they were most insistent that having a job had to come first. I trudged around with her, looking for restaurant work, but the reception given to a w̄oman who brings her child with her to an interview was quite negative, and the search proved fruitless.

So, too, was my check of publishers to whom I had sent articles. I had sent *Reader's Digest* a short true story about an old Murri woman who lived in the mangroves on the edge of town and the incredible life she had lived. When I rang to make an appointment, even the telephonist had read my story and she became upset about it on the phone. At the interview, however, I was informed that, although everyone there had been deeply touched by the story, it was felt that such stories about Aboriginal people were 'premature', their readership wasn't ready.

At *Pol* I was told the articles I had sent, in which I had proposed new ways of addressing feminist concerns, were good, but that they had chosen not to publish them. This, of course, was their prerogative. I was disappointed later to learn that my ideas had been reworked by another writer and published by *Pol* under her name. I was too green at the time to know what to do about something like that, but I felt ripped off.

Disheartened, but not willing to give up, I wrote a couple of topical articles and sent them to the *Australian*. I thought, I must stick with areas I know a lot about. So one of these new pieces was about a speech given by a visiting Native American which had direct parallels to concerns in Australia. The other was an analysis of an Aboriginal issue that had made news. A few days after sending them, I followed up with a phone call. I was invited to come in to discuss the work with an acting editor, Dominic Nagle.

Dominic wanted to talk with me outside the office and arranged for a staff member, a woman called Allison, to look after Naomi while we went to a small cafe nearby. Once seated, he told me we'd left the building because he wanted to be frank. Newspapers, he said, had been told by the government not to carry any more anti-apartheid or pro-Aboriginal coverage than they could help. Dominic disapproved of this interference with the 'free' press, but said his job was dependent on carrying out the paper's policies. My work, he told me, was great and he would have liked to run the pieces. When we returned to the office, I found Naomi clutching an envelope. Allison had written her a reference on *Australian* stationery for being such 'a good girl'.

I was amazed by what Dominic had said, though I appreciated the risk he had taken in telling me and the reasons behind his decision. He had said he wanted to contact me again in a few months because he liked my direct writing style, and I felt encouraged by this. However, beneath that feeling I was angry, very angry, that

ROBERTA SYKES

my efforts had been short-circuited, and I believed that the public was being manipulated by the government.

Up to this point I hadn't really thought much about government. Townsville was a long way from the federal centre of power. I had had little to do with local politicians, having left that aspect to people such as Evelyn Scott and Margaret Reynolds to deal with, both of whom knew much more about it than me. My two brushes with politics had been, one unremarkable, the other unimpressive: the Premier, Mr Joh Bjelke-Petersen, had held a function at Lowth's Hotel at which I'd organised the service of food and drinks; and Mr Killoran, who was in charge of Aboriginal Affairs for the state of Queensland, had once met with representatives from OPAL. During this meeting he had, in front of everyone, patted me on the knee and told me he could get me a house. I had almost fainted with embarrassment at his behaviour and everyone had been affronted on my behalf.

The thought grew in my mind that I'd have to fight Canberra if I wanted to get my work published. This was a tall order and I didn't have a clue where to start.

When the twelve weeks of Russel's term in boarding school were almost over I had made no progress towards either making a living or finding a place where we could all stay. In the terms of Margaret's lease she could not have children living in her flat, and Naomi had made the most of this once she'd twigged to it. When she didn't get her own way she would threaten to scream because, although she didn't understand the reasons why, Margaret and I had tried to impress on her the need to be quiet while we were at home. A Taurean,

Naomi could not be reasoned with or cajoled once she'd made up her mind.

William and I had agreed to meet at Aunty Glad's house to discuss our respective futures. I was concerned that he may have become angry and violent once he realised I was not going back to live with him, and Aunty Glad's presence would ensure this did not happen. William picked up Russel from school and they drove down to Brisbane. Naomi and I came up from Sydney by train.

Russel did not want to continue at boarding school. I felt, therefore, that both children should come with me, and that William should financially support them until I was able to do so.

William, however, had been going up to Charters Towers on weekends and taking Russel out fishing and camping, the very things he'd always baulked at doing while we were together. We had also earlier agreed, because of the very deep attachment they displayed towards each other, that we wouldn't separate the children. I was surprised when he said that Russel and Naomi were both to return to Townsville with him. Immediately I knew that this was a manipulative tactic designed to force me to return too. I refused.

I felt sure that William had neither the love nor the stamina to keep the children long term, so although I was sad to leave them with him, in my heart I knew it would not be for too long. I returned to Sydney.

I had spent my small store of cash and I was now desperate to find work. Margaret suggested I might find something at the Cahill's restaurant at the top of William Street, which was a short block from where she lived.

At this self-service restaurant, I was unhappy to find

myself just carrying loads of dirty plates from the tables to the kitchen, with little or no prospect of advancement. But at least I could contribute to the rent and pay for my share of the domestic expenses. I was biding my time. Margaret kept encouraging me to write, but I went through a very stressful period.

When I first arrived in Sydney I had visited the address Denis Walker had given me—a large house in Ruthven Street, Bondi Junction—to meet the people he had suggested I contact. The pace in the house was frenetic, with people coming and going, and Naomi had become distressed. Taking care of her had largely prevented me from absorbing much of what was happening around me, or of striking up anything in the way of a friendship or even a proper conversation.

Now, with more freedom, I sought out some of these people again, although I preferred to meet with them individually and away from the bustle of their house. I didn't hear well in noisy environments.

I was never sure who actually lived there. Sekai Holland, an extremely assertive woman from Rhodesia, and her husband certainly did, and some of the Murris (although, so they informed me, in New South Wales they use the word 'Koori') had clothes and bedrolls, so their nomadic lifestyle obviously included staying over at this house. But I also met a lot of white people living there who were active in many of the burning issues of the time, such as the anti-war movement, anti-apartheid, and support for the liberation struggle in Rhodesia.

One of the people I met, Neville Yeomans, a psychiatrist, was active and well-versed in the politics of most of the issues, and he began calling by to see me after he'd finished work. It eventuated that he had fallen in love with a North Vietnamese woman and was in the process of a very stressful divorce from his wife. He talked at great length about the trials of these family matters, so much so that I felt that I was his counsellor. But he also managed to give me a rundown on many important issues and generally kept me informed about the political activities that were taking place.

My youngest sister, Leonie, now had two sons and was living with her husband, Terry, just a few blocks away. Terry worked at a television station and his shifts were long and irregular. As Leonie was very advanced with her third pregnancy, I offered to stay for a couple of days to look after her two young boys while she went into hospital. When she returned, with three children well under school age, she was quite distracted. Even to go for a walk in the park, she looked like a procession with her stroller, a child hanging onto each side, nappy bag, bottles and spare changes for the toddlers who were also not yet toilet trained.

Nevertheless, visiting her helped soothe the ache in my heart as I was missing my own children. Also, I used her home as a postal address to receive letters from Townsville. Family and friends, including a Catholic priest, Father Kevin Livingstone, who lived in the presbytery across the street from William, wrote to me that William was making threats to harm me. So I didn't want to be easily found.

Strange things began happening around my work, my life at Margaret's flat and elsewhere. Often, pairs of suited white men, detectives I thought, followed me as I walked from home to Cahill's. Sometimes a pair would be sitting in a car, just watching me. I grew nervous and confided my fear to Margaret. At her suggestion I began to use some of my scarce resources to catch a cab home, even though it was only a few hundred metres away. I often finished work at around 10.30 or 11 pm, and in the dark I felt vulnerable and afraid, sensations I couldn't live with.

Then we found evidence that someone had been in the flat: papers not where we had left them, things rearranged. On one occasion we asked the woman across the hall if she had noticed anyone coming or going. 'Just a plumber, to fix your sink,' she replied. The sink didn't need repairs, and we hadn't reported any problems to the apartment block management. It was quite worrying.

Even more strangely, my mail, addressed to me care of Leonie, was also tampered with. Once she found an empty envelope for me in her letter-box, and the next day its contents were delivered to her house even though the pages did not contain her address. We were mystified.

One afternoon Margaret and I went into a bar in Darlinghurst Road which played loud music. Whenever I could, I still loved to dance, and dance music was always a magnet. The place was full of Americans on R&R from Vietnam, and almost immediately two of them began to try to strike up a conversation with us. Margaret, who was soon to become engaged to a South American, wasn't very interested in the rather rough-looking white soldier who spoke to her. However, his companion, a sober and tidy Black American, Charles, wanted to know what was happening in our struggle in Australia, and his concern about our issues interested me.

We became friends. He accompanied me to the Mosman home of Mrs Barrie Ovenden, who was then the editor of a publication funded by the Department of

Aboriginal Affairs, *Identity*. We all sat around and talked politics. We also visited the zoo as he wanted to see some of the unique Australian animals—koalas and kangaroos—which he had heard about.

I told Charles about the strange events that had been happening since I had made contact with the Black movement in Sydney. His work was in reconnaissance, so the things I was describing made sense to him where they had made none to me. Because I was new on the scene, he said, I was attracting the attention of secret service organisations, such as ASIO. They didn't need to dog people so thoroughly if they already knew them, because after a while they could almost predict their whereabouts and likely reactions at any given time or event. But with someone new, they needed to find out as much as possible about the person, their habits, their potential for violence, and so on.

His explanation made sense, and I was comforted by it, although I still didn't like what was happening.

Charles was a very sensitive person and he soon picked up on how nervously I flinched from any gesture of affection. 'Are you alright?' he asked me many times. Towards the end of his brief R&R leave I felt he deserved some explanation for the rigidity and quick wall of coldness he met when he extended even ordinary courtesies, such as taking my arm protectively to cross the street. We had shared a lot during his visit; he had talked about many of his concerns regarding the situation of racism in both the USA and Vietnam, and I had tested on him some of the ideas I was developing about how things should progress here.

So, I found myself telling Charles of my fear of men, of their intentions, and of the gang-rape from which my fears stemmed. He was kind and solicitous, as I had intuitively known he would be, and we made a pact that he would share this knowledge with no one. When he left to return to the war, and later to his wife and family in America, I felt extremely alone. I had known very few people to whom I felt sufficiently close or trusted enough to share my awful secret. I had found a security in telling someone outside of my everyday life, a safety in the knowledge that Charles would never be able to use the information against me. It was critically important that no one could drop a careless word in conversation anywhere near my son, something Charles would never be in a position to do. After he left we corresponded for several years.

At around this time I learned from other Blacks that they were being harassed by ASIO and by the police. Some of the emerging leaders were being picked up and charged with morals offences. I became alarmed, and on a few occasions, when detectives stopped and questioned me for no apparent reason, I would be very short and direct with them in response.

'Is it your intention to arrest me?' I would ask. 'If so, on what charge? And if not, leave me alone.'

People in the movement were preparing to go to Canberra for what they told me was the People's Parliament. They invited me to be one of the speakers. I had no idea what to expect and had never been to Canberra, but the current was running in that direction and these colleagues were offering transport. In order to accept I would have to throw in my job, but that seemed no great sacrifice. Scraping plates had kept me from participating in the day to day work of the movement. It was time to move on.

I remember little of what happened during that time

in Canberra. It was warm and sunny. I was impressed with the organisation and camaraderie displayed throughout the day, and very nervous about speaking in front of so many people. When my name was called to come to the platform, which had been erected on the lawns outside Parliament House, my legs were shaking so much that I could barely walk. After I gave my speech, without notes but on ideas that I had thought a lot about, I received hearty applause and was warmly congratulated. I was surprised anyone had even heard me because my knees had made such a racket, knocking together the whole time.

But this was it, the day of my declaration. I had stood up to be counted amongst those people who wished to change society. I had spoken up against racism and demanded an end to this evil. If ASIO officers were to follow me now, I thought, they might think they had good reason.

Instead of travelling back to Sydney, I organised a lift to Melbourne. I was offered accommodation in a summer house behind a big house in Murrumbeena occupied by several lectures from Monash University. However, it eventuated that they never did clear the junk out of it and I was obliged to live in the house. I had no income and in return for sharing their food, I cooked and waged war against the grime they had allowed to accumulate in the lounge, bathroom and kitchen, setting traps to catch the mice which threatened to infest their larder.

Neal Barrett, a lecturer in economics who shared the house, had quite a political mind. Certainly he knew a great deal about politics and was happy to share that information with me. I had not previously heard many of the expressions that were part of everyday conversation in the south, or so it seemed to me. The terms 'left wing' and 'right wing' confused me; I knew they were descriptive of something but was unable to sort out just what. Neal enlightened me.

How politically naive I was during those early days. I used my leisure time wisely, reading almost everything I could find in their house, though the dense tomes on economic theory defied me.

One day I was surprised and delighted to receive a letter from Cheryl Buchanan, whom I had met in Brisbane at the offices of the National Tribal Council. She asked me to contact a man, Ian Sturzaker, who had promised to give the Gurindji People a truck. I was to find out what progress had been made in this regard. Her letter ended with a cryptic sentence: 'We all thought you were very brave when you were talking to Denis.'

I was later to learn that a woman had chipped Denis for swearing and, by way of response, he had assaulted her. She'd been taken to the hospital and given stitches. The very next night I had come in to the head-quarters and done the same thing, even stretching my luck to insist that Denis not strike his foot out towards the child playing on the floor. This explained the silence that had fallen over the room after I had spoken. Had I known about the earlier event, I'm not sure that I would have been so quick to speak. It's easy to be brave when you don't realise you are in any danger.

I paid a call on Ian Sturzaker; he was a merchant banker with a neat office off a laneway in the heart of Melbourne. Ian was pleased to see me and told me a remarkable story. He had read in the newspapers about the Gurindji strike on Wave Hill which, by that time, had been going for many years. In 1966 the Gurindji had moved to Wattie Creek, where they were trying to establish themselves. They needed a truck to enable them to fetch supplies and to get to work erecting a fence around the area that they were demanding be excised for them, with fencing supplied by supportive trade union members.

Ian had been struck by the courage of these Aboriginal people, by their determination to stick to their demands against all comers. He had written to say he would organise a truck for them. He'd planned to ask a few people in his social and economic circles to throw in a thousand dollars each; thirty or forty people ought to have done, he thought. It was money none of them would really miss. But when the time came for him to shake the tin and ask his mates, he became shy. So, having made the commitment, he had purchased the truck himself.

He explained this with an air of great embarrassment, then turned the conversation to me. Who was I and what was I doing? As he had been frank and open with me, I told him I had come south with the intention of being a writer, but that my plans weren't panning out.

'Can you write?' he asked me with a directness I found quite unnerving.

'Yes. I'm a good writer. I just haven't been able to get anything published,' I replied.

He mused for a moment, then picked up the phone. 'Have you heard of *The Review*?' he asked. I had. 'Well, the editor, Richard, owes me a favour. I'll get him to have a look at your work.'

He rang Richard Walsh who, on that day, was in Sydney. When would he be back in Melbourne? Lunch on Thursday? Friday? Which day, he asked, would be good for me?

And so it was that I met Richard Walsh and he made a commitment to Ian to look at my work. Throughout the meal they talked of people and things about which I knew nothing, so I was quite bored. Only at the end, as the table was being cleared, did they turn their attention to me. 'Send three pieces over to the office,' said Richard, 'and I'll have a look at them.'

On the next working day I brought in the three articles, searching out the address on the map I carried with me everywhere, and left them with the receptionist, then went home to wait.

I heard nothing that week, nor the following week, and was becoming disheartened. However, two weekends later, The Review came out and one of my articles was in it. I was beside myself with happiness.

I expected to hear something from the paper, but no one contacted me. The following weekend's paper carried a second article, after which I received a phone call.

'I'm calling from The Review. Have you got your column ready yet?' a male voice, not Richard, asked. 'And we want to talk about getting a block made for your name.'

I was on my way, I thought excitedly. I rang Ian to thank him, and was invited out to dinner to celebrate.

Around this same time I had been hearing and reading about a police chase that was underway in Western Australia. A forty-year-old Aboriginal man, Lionel Brockman, his wife, Jean, aged thirty-five, and their eleven children—the oldest, Reg, was aged eighteen— were being pursued across the desert and, according to the newspapers, were leading police on a merry chase.

As I sought out more information, I became appalled by the terrible unfairness of this situation. The state authorities were spending more money chasing this man and his family than Brockman's crimes warranted. He was wanted only for a series of minor thefts. I carefully scanned everything about the story, because I did not want to find myself inadvertently supporting a criminal with some violent charge against him which hadn't been made public. However, once I learned that he had no prior record I felt moved to do something to help him. But what?

Neal and the other men in the house were helpful with suggestions. Lionel Brockman would need money, they told me, to help meet the costs of his defence once he was caught. Many people had already read about the case and I could sense a wave of public sympathy for him, so I began to go around to union offices to inquire if they would assist. I also organised a central place that people could contact or through which anyone who felt similarly moved could channel funds to the Brockmans.

The Lionel Brockman Defence Fund was born, and soon even a demonstration had been planned. There was no way to contact Mr Brockman to let him know how much support there was for him. However, at our demonstration an effigy of the WA Premier was burned and that made news even in Perth.

I had only one pair of shoes, boots they were, and at this time they wore out. They were seven years old. My only income was the small payments I received from my articles in *The Review*, which I spent on food and other basic necessities. So, when I went looking for shoes to replace my old ones, I found them to be far beyond my resources. A friend suggested I should look

in an Army disposal store, where they sold very cheap
sturdy boots. I was pleased to find a pair which fitted
me, though they were thick-soled and military-looking.

Hence I came to be wearing these boots at the
Lionel Brockman support demonstration, and photos
of me so attired were flashed to newspapers around the
country. I was gaining a reputation for militancy, I felt,
based, to some extent, on my footwear.

I cadged lifts and travelled around, attending conferences, speaking to groups and raising public awareness.
During a conference in Canberra people were asked to
participate in a 'Free Angela Davis' demonstration outside the US Embassy. (Angela Davis, a Black American,
was being held in isolation in a US prison, charged with,
and later acquitted of, kidnap and murder.) I attended
along with everyone else, and a photographer, no doubt
attracted by my afro hairstyle, snapped my picture
as I held up a placard. This photo was published on
the cover of *Tribune*, the Communist Party newspaper,

leading many people to believe, erroneously, that I was a member of the Communist Party.

Around the same time, Denis Walker and others were in the process of setting up a group called the Australian Black Panther Party, modelled on the American Panthers whose militancy had dominated much of the television coverage from the US. As I had little to do with this, I don't know if Denis' group had an affiliation with its namesake or just adopted the name from the material the members were reading, although I suspect the latter. This development, which was trumpeted by the local media around the personae of Denis, Gary Foley and Billy Craigie, created a great deal of fear in the white community, and caused just about anyone involved in the struggle to be regarded as 'Black Power'.

As I supported the philosophy of liberation by whatever means necessary, I did not divorce myself from the politics of Black Power, and I explained my understanding of this philosophy later in a published debate, 'Black Power in Australia', with the then Senator, Neville Bonner. Even Neville, in his counter-argument, wrote that there was 'good Black Power' and 'bad Black Power', and that he was for the former, demonstrating the difficulty which people had in allocating specific meaning to the concept.

My housemates in Melbourne began to report interference with the phone, and again I often felt that I was being followed. We would see men sitting in cars on the street outside the house. One rainy day we were sitting in the lounge, one of the housemates was playing the piano, when another who was looking out a window spied a man in a raincoat standing just outside the room. The house was set well back from the street and was almost completely concealed by a tall hedge right across the front, so no one would have been standing there by accident. One of the guys said the man was soaked through and looked miserable, and he thought he would invite him in for a cup of tea. When he opened the door, the raincoated man ran up the driveway, and shortly we heard a car taking off. After this incident we made sport of the probability of our being under surveillance.

Lionel Brockman was finally arrested after a chase which had lasted weeks. He had been dubbed the 'Desert Fox' and the 'Desert Houdini' by the press for his ability to elude capture. The state had put up helicopters and small planes, searching the thin ribbons of road which criss-crossed the otherwise almost completely empty plains. We found out when he was scheduled to appear in court and Neal, his sister Jenny and I determined to go.

Meanwhile I had been regularly in touch with William and Mum who, still with Arthur, had shut the shop and moved to Brisbane to be closer to her sister, Aunty Glad. Mum and Arthur frequently shuttled backwards and forwards between Brisbane and the north so that Mum could keep an eye on her houses, maintain her friendships and visit William, Russel and Naomi. From William and Mum I learned that Russel did not seem to be coping well with his separation from me. I asked if I could have the children with me for the holidays, though I had no idea how I would be able to support them. William replied that he would only let Russel come, and then only for a short stay. Naomi was 'his' and he didn't intend to let me see her.

The morning of Russel's arrival coincided with the day we were due to depart on the long journey across the Nullarbor Desert to Perth. I recall Russel's little face as he disembarked from the plane and walked up the hallway, peering anxiously around to see if I was there to meet him. I have no idea what William may have told him, but he looked terribly serious and very concerned. He was just ten years old. His eyes lit up when he saw me, and he was comforted by my presence. I didn't know how he would react when I told him that we weren't staying in Melbourne, but were leaving immediately to drive to Perth.

I had missed the little man, and it almost broke my heart to see him already looking so worried, well before his time. But as for our impending journey, it didn't matter because wherever I was Russel just wanted to be. Once he was seated in the car he started talking, and he talked his way almost non-stop across the desert. We were splitting the driving into shifts and Russel's constant chatter, of his ideas and things that had happened in Townsville, initially disturbed the off-driver who needed to sleep.

'Russel, William wrote to me that you were withdrawn. He said you hardly ever talked any more,' I said.

'Mummy, I've been saving it up for you!' he replied, and happily launched into yet another anecdote from his life and times at school.

When my companions heard this, they smiled. They were then happy to tolerate his young, excited voice going on and on in the background while they slept.

We drove all that day, and throughout the night, arriving in Perth the following afternoon when we went immediately to the office of Jack Davis. Jack, who was already well-known as a poet and local organiser, had indicated his willingness to help us. On our arrival he made arrangements for us to stay at an Aboriginal hostel. Neal and Jenny, although both white, were also welcome to stay at the hostel, which surprised and pleased them enormously.

We held meetings attended by many local people, as well as attending court on the appointed day. Following his arrest I had written to Lionel, and he had replied, and through our correspondence he knew we intended to make every effort to be there to support him.

Lionel was a tall, well-built and handsome Black man with the most brilliant sparkling blue eyes, very protective towards his petite wife and immensely proud of his children. His story was simple. After working his entire adult life in a variety of jobs in rural areas, Lionel had been laid off and unable to find more work. For the first time in his life he'd been reduced to going, stony broke, into a government office to seek Aboriginal welfare. He had had to beg donations of small cans of petrol along the way to get there.

Leaving his family outside in the car, sweltering and starved, he had gone into the office where he was interrogated by a white woman in a condescending manner. Instead of relief he was given advice: Go out and get a job.

I was incensed—this had come from a woman who was being paid a living wage out of the Aboriginal budget, supposedly employed to assist Aboriginal people. It reminded me, too, of my own experience, years before in Newcastle when I had been embarrassed and distressed about having to plead a case for poverty in front of a stranger. I had come away with a food order. Lionel, with all those children to feed, had received nothing but an affront for his pain.

That night, after his interview, he knocked a flimsy door to a store off its brackets and helped himself to some groceries. He repeated this crime in several country towns as he travelled around looking for work. It was pitiful to sit in the court and hear different store-keepers, who had been flown down for the trial and were being accommodated at government expense, give the judge lists of the items they had found missing: baby food, cans of powdered milk, bandaids. This was the nature of the crimes Lionel had committed.

After court, I met Lionel and Jean. Like many others, I was amazed by Lionel's skills and bushcraft in eluding the police. (A police report had told that Lionel's vehicle had broken down and, with the few tools he had, he'd converted the truck from automatic to manual transmission to keep it going.)

'The police—they could have found me. They had every waterhole staked out. They knew where I was,' he told me.

'So why didn't they catch you?'

'They were being paid double and triple time. Why would they want to catch me?' he replied.

One night, he said, he had walked behind a small group of police playing cards near a waterhole to fill up his canteen. They knew he was there, and he knew they knew. He thought they would take him then, he was so close he could see the cards that they were holding. But no, they had all studiously avoided glancing up to see him.

When at last the police caught him, they beat him, he said. They blamed him because the Force had been embarrassed by the publicity the case had generated. The press had estimated that about half a million dollars had been spent in the search.

I reiterated to Lionel that there was money in the fund we had established on his behalf to help him out. He said he preferred to go with the lawyers the state had provided. He wanted his wife to receive the money because, as he was to be sentenced, she'd be doing it tough to keep the family together in his absence.

It was Christmas 1971, and we were pleased when we went around to the house where Jean was staying with friends or relatives and were able to give her some money.

That Christmas, too, Russel spent his allowance on buying a set of Tweed perfume and talc, the first real gift he'd ever purchased for me, apart from toy cars and the like which he'd presented me with in the past. My little boy was growing up.

In Sydney and Melbourne, since the referendum, it had been possible for Blacks to go into a hotel and have a drink. Some hotels still discriminated against us by refusing us entry, and these were battles we had yet to take on, but generally speaking we were served.

In Perth, however, it was back to the bad old days. Neal, Jenny and I went to a number of places where they were admitted but I was refused. Some friends we had made then told us of a hotel that would serve us. We went there, and yes, they would sell us a drink—but we'd have to stand around in the backyard to drink it.

We also learned that WA state laws prohibited Aboriginal people from crossing the state borders, and non-Aboriginal people were not permitted to transport them. Fortunately these laws were not rigidly enforced, or we would never have been able to arrive there in order to receive the publicans' refusals!

A few years later, a Sydney-based Wiradjeri Elder, Shirley Smith (MumShirl), would also visit Western Australia and be refused service from a range of places, including cafes and accommodation houses. A diabetic in need of regular meals, she was compelled by one of these refusals to forgo her medication. She complained to the local unions, which threatened to cut off the water and power to the businesses concerned.

I recall people in those days would frequently ask me why I was an activist. They often didn't understand when I told them that we just wanted to be treated decently.

6

When I'd reluctantly put Russel on a plane back to Townsville after we had returned from Perth, I cadged a ride with some priests who were driving to Sydney. I checked in with Leonie and Margaret, but basically my intention was to pursue news in the Black community. I needed to stay in touch with events as they unfolded in order to keep my *Review* articles relevant and up-to-date. I visited the Aboriginal Legal Service (ALS), a shopfront office which offered free legal advice to Kooris. It had been modelled on an idea from the Black Panthers in America, so Denis Walker had informed me. At the time most Kooris just pleaded guilty to anything they were charged with, for a variety of reasons including misunderstanding of the charges against them, unfamiliarity with the legal process and no access to legal advice.

There was also talk of establishing a medical service along the same lines, with volunteer staff, to provide badly needed attention for sick Aboriginal people. I was taken by the vibrancy and enthusiasm of many of the people concerned, including Gordon Briscoe, Naomi

Mayers, Paul Coe and the two Garys, Williams and Foley.

Leonie had, by this time, moved out of her city flat to a house in Epping. I had never warmed to her husband, but whenever I was in Sydney I stayed with them, giving Leonie some assistance and company because Terry was away so often. While I was there I packed my clothes into two small suitcases, which I called 'summer' and 'winter', as I was now ready to live a nomadic life in an effort to track down news.

After a few days I returned to Melbourne to keep tabs on the Brockman Defence Fund and find out how to send copy into *The Review* office from elsewhere. Then I travelled back to Sydney once more. I was pleasantly surprised when I was brusquely confronted by Naomi Mayers as I was checking out some information with people at the Clifton Hotel, one of two hotels frequented by Blacks in Redfern. She asked me where I had been during the intervening week.

'Why? Why do you want to know?' I asked guardedly.

'Because we needed you here. We looked all over for you, we needed something written, something you could have done. We know you write for that newspaper. Well, you can write for us too!' she replied.

The reason for my pleasure at these remarks is that it is often quite difficult for new people to penetrate cliques, and even more so when the members are all under enormous pressure and scrutiny from outside. The group of community activists who were in the process of setting up a range of services for the Black community had, of course, attracted the attention of ASIO and the police. How were they to know that any newcomer was not a 'spy'?

I wrote on a range of Black community issues,

particularly the plight of Aboriginal cotton-chippers in the fields around Wee Waa. They were on strike for better pay and conditions: their health and lives were under threat from aerial spraying in this chemical-intensive industry. As well, I attended numerous meetings to plan new services and strategies.

It was in the office of the newly established Aboriginal Medical Service (AMS) that I first met MumShirl, whose awesome reputation had preceded our meeting. I had heard so many good things about this woman, but recently I had heard that she had been critical of me. Despite my fear of her reputation, which included smacking people down when they crossed her, I decided to give her the opportunity to size me up in person and for me to do likewise.

I asked her to step into the backroom so we could have some privacy, and then I put to her the rumours I had heard. She sat quietly for a moment and then, denying the rumours, she asked me to consider whether or not she would have made the comments that were being attributed to her: that I was an upstart and that I was leaping into the media spotlight from out of nowhere. She proceeded to list everything she knew about me: that I was from Townsville and had two children, my involvement with OPAL, my work for *The Review*, and my initiation of a support, publicity and defence structure for Lionel Brockman. I was impressed, given that we hadn't met before, but still wary.

We agreed to work together for our common cause and the benefit of the community. It was not long, however, before we had won each other's respect, and eventually she began to introduce me to people as her 'daughter'. The first time she did that, she drew me aside later and said that she hoped I didn't mind. I said I felt honoured.

I had learned that a conference was to be held at the University of Queensland in Brisbane, and I made preparations to attend. On my arrival I realised I had already met most of the main Black activists and speakers who were present. On 26 January 1972, when we were into perhaps the second day of the meeting, a rumour began to sweep through the crowd: an 'Aboriginal Embassy' had been set up on the lawn across the road from Parliament House in Canberra, they needed our support.

The idea, an Embassy for us Black Australians, who knew that even foreigners had more representation than us, was very exciting. Bruce McGuinness, from Victoria, offered me a lift, but I was reluctant to accept. He had driven me to the Aboriginal Advancement League when I was in Melbourne, and I'd found him to have a lead foot. He realised why I was demurring and immediately volunteered to travel at a reasonable speed. He drove a big eight-cylinder car, packed full of people, and as soon as we were ready we set off.

It's impossible to adequately describe the ad hoc operation of the Embassy and the emotions that we all shared. By the time we arrived the beach umbrella that had constituted the Embassy for the first few hours had been replaced with a small tent. When large numbers of supporters began to roll into Canberra, local people supplied even more tents and, within a few days, we had the beginnings of a small tent city.

We were very apprehensive that the police would arrest us immediately, but the truth, when it came out over the next few days, added mirth to our emotional mix. At the time, the Northern Territory was just that, a territory, administered by politicians and public servants in Canberra, and containing quite large sections of Crown land. The government had framed a law that there was to be no camping on Crown land. However, because Crown land in the Northern Territory was home to dispossessed Aboriginal people who had nowhere else to live, this law specifically excluded Aborigines. The expanse of land in front of Parliament House was also Crown land, but it had obviously never entered the minds of the politicians that Aborigines would set up camp there.

And set up camp we did. There was a lot of work to be done and many willing workers. Just organising cups of tea and cleaning up afterwards was a chore, because we were situated a fair walk from the toilet block, our only access to water. There was no shower block, of course, so local people came by each day and picked up small groups of us to take to their houses where we could wash.

People from all over Australia began sending small contributions towards the support of our Embassy goal. Very few of those staffing the Embassy had any other means of support and generally our funds were very low. Most of the people involved, including myself, were without transport. Blacks in general could not afford cars. Simple tasks such as bringing in food—bread, sugar and cool drinks—required us to walk long distances.

It became apparent from the breadth of support we received, mainly from the kindly folk of Canberra, that we would have to start producing leaflets to tell people what we were doing and the reasons behind our actions, if we didn't want to have to repeat this information several hundred times a day.

Five years had passed since the referendum in 1967, which had acknowledged Aboriginal citizenship, but still little had changed. Some states, notably Queensland and Western Australia, continued to have their own laws relating to Aborigines, many of whom were still confined on reserves and missions, and required passes handed out by white managers in order to go into the nearest town.

We all knew the conditions on these places were appalling and at last we had found the means by which, we hoped, to bring about desperately needed change. Black people, including children, were dying of starvation and neglect, out of earshot and view of the majority of white citizens who lived in the cities. We were excited by the prospect of throwing the truth out to the media so that everyone could look at it and make up their own minds. This was largely the mission that we took onto ourselves.

Tasks were allocated according to people's skills and depending on who was present at any time. I was elected to be the Embassy's First Secretary, in charge of generating information sheets—but our jobs were not exclusive. John Newfong, whom I had met in Brisbane many moons ago and who was then living mainly in Sydney, also shared some of the written work, and we were both required by circumstances also to be tea-makers, bottle-washers and carriers of water. Some people, including Chika Dixon who worked on the waterside, travelled up and down to Canberra from Sydney, Brisbane and Melbourne by train on their days off to take part.

Most of us took the mission we had set ourselves very seriously. The original idea had been hatched in Sydney by Kevin Gilbert, but he was on parole and not allowed to leave that city's limits. Kevin had found some willing bodies to undertake the Embassy's establishment, but he later told me that he had no idea at the time that the spark of his idea would be fanned by the strong winds of discontent and support, and blown into a major fire which would irrevocably bring change across the country.

'Go out and publicise,' was a common refrain, and one I took quite earnestly. Apart from writing about what was happening, I felt that, since most Aboriginal people couldn't afford newspapers, it was incumbent upon us to go to them and share with them what we were hoping to do.

I visited as many places as I could to spread the word. As the weather grew colder in Canberra my health suffered and I was treated for bronchitis and respiratory infections several times. Leonie must have grown tired of my comings and goings, often at strange hours in the middle of the night, to exchange the suitcase I was carrying according to my next destination. Like almost everyone else involved, I cadged lifts whenever possible, slept on floors and ate whatever I could scrounge.

We were all obviously under surveillance. No doubt there were those in positions of power who thought that we were a threat to national security, and didn't see our bid for a decent way of life as a saving grace for a whole lot of desperately unhappy people.

Some politicians supported our efforts though, taking different ones over to join them for a meal in the parliamentary dining room. I met quite a few people that way. An election was looming at the end of the year and some, particularly Labor, politicians recognised that by our actions we had put Aboriginal issues firmly on the agenda. Also, as we were moving about the countryside visiting communities, we were encouraging our people to enrol to vote.

At the Embassy we were often buoyed by the media attention we received. As well as featuring the Embassy, they began to delve into conditions in which Aboriginal people lived, in an effort to highlight some of the issues that we were protesting against. This was the first time these conditions were given any in-depth or comprehensive attention, and we would have been quite pleased even if this was all our work had achieved.

Ian Sturzaker was one of many people in unlikely places who turned out to be very supportive. He had organised for me to meet Ranald McDonald, editor at *The Age*, in the hope that I might find some casual employment with the paper. When that failed, however, Ian promised me a hand-held loud hailer Ranald had once given him. The image of smartly dressed Ian, merchant banker, flying first class to Sydney carrying a loud hailer caused mirth amongst the Black movement and his own wealthy associates whenever they were told.

At various times, Ian had introduced me to some of his friends and colleagues; among them were Margaret and Leon Fink, Sandra and David Bardas, and a solicitor, Eric Strasser, all of whom were to play important roles over the ensuing years.

Ian rang one day and found me wracked with bronchitis for the second time in two weeks. The next time we met he put forward a proposition. I needed a safe, warm and dry place in which to recover between these jaunts to Canberra and around the country, he said, acknowledging what we both knew—that my light sleeping bag was little protection in the capital city's freezing conditions. He was prepared to provide such a place for me on certain conditions. His stipulations were that I would use the place primarily to keep all my things together and to get on with my writing. He would be unhappy if I let the place become a crash pad for the many homeless people he realised I knew. I agreed. When he asked me which city I wanted it to be in, I said Sydney. I sensed his disappointment as he had a much wider circle of friends and acquaintances in Melbourne whom he thought I could tap for support on behalf of the Embassy. Nevertheless, he agreed and said he'd have a couple of places ready for me to look at next time I was in Sydney.

The first place I visited was perfect. A bedsitter, it consisted of only one large room with a bathroom and kitchenette attached. Located in Crown Street, Surry Hills, I was just a short walk from Redfern and the city. Eric Strasser had referred me to the real estate agent who managed the block, so I didn't have to anticipate problems with the landlord. As the flat was unfurnished, Eric offered to supply basic living and work furniture—a bed, wardrobe and desk—at his own expense as his contribution to the struggle.

One of the main reasons I was so pleased to have a space of my own was that, ever since the rape, I had developed a series of compulsive behaviours. The privacy of single accommodation allowed me to indulge in them without raising comment from others. I showered six, sometimes more times a day, and felt the need to wash my hands upwards of thirty or more times daily. Outside the flat I was drawn to sources of water—public taps, ladies' rooms and even bubblers—in which to wash my hands. Although I had few clothes, I changed into clean outfits often during the day, always carefully washing the clothes I'd just removed even though I hadn't worn them long enough for them to have become soiled. I refused to put any of my clothes into washing machines, washing them all by hand in a plastic bucket. Despite this obsessive emphasis on cleanliness, I never felt clean.

I also felt ignorant and spent much of my time reading. I owned no radio or television, which may have provided a distraction, instead preferring the written word. With little cash to outlay on this obsession, I picked up any book or paper anyone else laid down, even pilfering newspapers left on trains or buses and carrying them off like a prize to read alone at home. I had developed a passion for reading mystery novels, murder stories and the like. I gained a great deal of pleasure from reading about bad guys who had hurt others being caught and punished, even though they were fictional characters.

By this time I had many regular readers of, and commentors on, my *Review* column. Frequently they expressed their opinion that other newspapers were doing the public a disservice by not having Blacks writing on these issues. *The Review* had a comparatively small, though committed, readership, and its editors felt that news from inside the struggle could best be supplied by Blacks and should enjoy a much wider readership.

So much was happening during this period that it's impossible to record all the events. Police in Redfern were carrying out regular raids on houses and hotels lived in or frequented by Blacks, and making many, and indiscriminate, arrests. Their activities caught the attention of civil liberties groups as well as priests, brothers and nuns from the Catholic Church. Sister

Ignatius from St Vincent's Hospital, Darlinghurst, who was over eighty years old, became a very active protester during this time, and was well-known for chasing after police officers during their rampages and recording their badge numbers. Many police began to remove their badges prior to raids in their efforts to become anonymous in their misdeeds.

Although not an everyday occurrence, police broke down the doors to houses in the middle of the night. Their only reason was because of the occupants' political activities. When we were pulled up by police on the street, we were often told we were 'well-known troublemakers'. This type of harassment caused us all to grow wary and secretive, even as we intensified our efforts to bring our community's conditions out for the scrutiny of the public.

Possibly because they realised they had unofficial police sanction, racist and anti-Aboriginal groups stepped up their activities against us. When we held meetings that were advertised in advance, it was not unusual to find thugs waiting for us as we left. On occasions when Blacks were bashed by these thugs, police often took hours to respond to our calls. On the weekend that I published an article in The Review about the harassment we were facing, its Sydney office was broken into and ransacked, and swastikas were painted on the walls and scrawled across their cheque books.

Often MumShirl and I went together to speak to white groups about the needs of the Medical Service, the Black community generally, and what we were hoping to achieve by the Embassy. After one such meeting early in the process, while we were having a cup of tea with the women who had invited us, one woman asked me what my tribal affiliations were. I replied that I had none that I was aware of.

Later, MumShirl took me to task. She said she had heard that I was telling people I wasn't Aboriginal, and asked if I knew how much this insulted Aboriginal people? 'Well,' I replied, 'I can't prove that I am. I have reason to think I am, but I can't prove it.'

'But,' said MumShirl, 'can you prove that you're not?'

When I said that I couldn't prove anything either way, that my mother was secretive about her own ancestry and had given me a pack of different stories about who my father was, MumShirl said that I was *choosing* not to be Aboriginal. This caused me to reflect deeply on my own motives. Did I not want to be aligned with people whom my own mother had so negatively portrayed? Was I constantly reacting against the mantra of evil, 'Abo. Abo. Just a fucking boong!', which had been thrown up by one of my attackers at his trial? Or was I trying to establish a separate, and in some way 'special', category just for myself?

I agonised over these questions. MumShirl had a way of getting to the very heart of a matter, and her decision to inform me of the pain I was causing bothered me acutely. How many others, I wondered, had I insulted with my posturing? Was there any way to find out? And how could I correct any damage I may have done?

Again I tried to prise information from my mother. I insisted that I *had* to know, that other people were asking me and I wanted to be able to answer. 'Roberta,' Mum said, 'have you asked these other people for something? How come they think they have a right to know your business, and mine?'

'No, Mum, I've asked for nothing,' I replied.

But of course I had. By my actions I was asking for a place in the struggle, for the opportunity to fight and, if necessary, to die, for what we believed in—equality, decency and a fair go. I had had enough of the way we were all being treated, and I didn't want my children, or any Black children, to live the way I had been forced to as a young person. The hardship, discrimination and violence I had faced in my youth had taken their toll, and I felt no price, not even life itself, was too high to pay for change.

I sometimes felt that I had been placed in a position where I had to choose between MumShirl and my own mother; this feeling was heightened when Mum saw a television program in which MumShirl introduced me as her daughter. Mum said she was very sorry if she was an embarrassment to me, sorry if she was not a 'MumShirl', and began to cry. I thought of the woman who had run with me in her arms over the hill in the middle of the night in an effort to save my life, the woman who had stood so firmly by me throughout the dark days following the rape and throughout the trials, and whose motivation was that she feared for my life and the lives of my children. I held my tongue and con-soled her. But I thought, too, of the hardships MumShirl had faced throughout her life and her own valiant struggle for survival. She lived with danger every day, the same sort of threat I lived under, and my iden-tification with her was all but absolute.

Although my flat was tiny, it was very convenient. As well as using it for work, from time to time the second single bed was pressed into service, despite Ian's admonition to the contrary. Travellers, I decided, es-pecially those coming through from Queensland, would be welcomed—such visits would keep me up to date with what was happening in my home state.

Denis Walker had gained a reputation amongst Sydney Blacks for his unpredictable anger and outbursts, and although his brilliance was always welcomed at meetings people shied away from offering him accommodation. I had no such difficulty with him and, contrary to what others told me, I found him to always be a gentleman when I was around. Much to my colleagues' surprise perhaps, he stayed at my flat several times. I made the house rules explicit, no alcohol, drugs, or dalliance, and he complied. He seemed grateful, I think, just to have a friend on whom he could rely. We discussed many things.

My flat, I am sure, was kept under surveillance. I received a phone call one day from Eric Strasser, who wanted to meet me in town. Two detectives, he said, had called on my renting agent, quizzing him about me in a manner designed to raise his curiosity, bring me into disrepute and have me evicted. The agent had contacted Eric immediately. Eric was concerned that when the police realised their tactics had not brought about the desired result, they might think up some way to harass me further or even to arrest me. We made plans to guard against this possibility. I was grateful for his friendship and concern.

Camaraderie amongst those of us who were active at the Embassy was high, but this is not to say that we didn't have discipline problems occasionally. We'd set rules, to which we had all agreed—no alcohol, drugs or casual sexual dalliances, particularly of an inter-racial nature, were to be tolerated. Of course there were always, as in any group, isolated cases where people broke the rules. Chicka Dixon and I often rotated between us the responsibility of going to Canberra 'to straighten up the camp' when we heard of these infractions.

Throwing my energies into these political activities meant I had little time to brood about my children. I missed them every day, but we were confronting enormous difficulties, politically and economically, and I was often glad that they were not exposed to these problems.

Mum, however, was increasingly unhappy about my activities, though she insisted she was concerned only for my safety. From time to time, death threats were made against those of us who were prominently associated with the Embassy, both individually and collectively. I wrote to Mum pointing out that I had been in much greater danger before, as I had been raped and near murdered when we weren't making waves, and that if we backed off things would just revert to those bad old days.

Mum wrote, 'I know you think you know what you are doing, dear, but remember what happened to Martin Luther King?'

I responded, 'Yes, Mum, and I'll try to keep more than a cardboard placard between me and the bad guys. Okay?' But Mum was not placated.

Another conference was called in Brisbane and I had been asked to go there in advance to assist with its organisation. Mum had moved to Labrador, a little township just north of Surfers Paradise, where she and Arthur were living in a caravan park. I decided to visit her to assure her that I was well.

However, just as I was about to leave Sydney, word came in that a death-list had been posted. Pastor Brady's church in Brisbane had already been bombed, and the lives of key organisers around the conference were threatened and my name was on the list. I was, as usual, almost broke, so I couldn't afford to sit around idle at Mum's place instead of going on to team up with the other conference organisers.

'What are you doing here, dear?' Mum greeted me.

'Just come by to see you, Mum,' I replied.

'Yes, and . . .' said Mum sceptically.

'Well, I thought I'd get a job here for a while.'

'I thought you were a journalist in Sydney,' Mum said, trying to get her head around this sudden turn of events.

'I am, Mum, but I think it would be fun to work here for a while. I'll look for a job as a waitress. It will give me something more to write about.'

'You've already *been* a waitress, Roberta. Is there anything you want to tell me?'

I gambled that it would be unlikely she would hear about these latest death threats and I didn't want her to worry unnecessarily. I also thought that whatever fools had put out the death list were unlikely to have any idea of my family ties, would not know where to find me, and that my presence at her place would not endanger her. So I said no.

The next day I put on a little straight-haired black wig, which I had packed at the last moment, and went out looking for a job. I found one at a seaside hotel not too far from the caravan park. Arthur would pass it every day on his way to his new hairdressing premises, so he could drive me in and pick me up.

The hotel manager walked around all day with two Doberman dogs at his side. I was mortified—snakes and dogs don't mix. I hadn't seen them when I applied for the job, otherwise I wouldn't have taken it. The work wasn't difficult, though I spent a lot of energy keeping some distance between myself and the dogs. Fortunately, the manager's wife mainly ran the dining facility and he ran the bar, so I 'imagined' the presence of the dogs far more often than I actually saw them.

One day I received a card from the post office, telling me I had a parcel to collect. I had asked Neil, in Melbourne, to forward my boots on to me at Mum's as I thought I would need them in the cooler weather.

I could find nowhere to park outside the post office so I asked Mum to get the parcel while I sat double-parked. Through the large glass window I saw the man place the parcel on the counter and Mum, unaware that I could see her, bent down and put her ear to the parcel before picking it up. When she came out, she walked gingerly and carried the parcel at arm's length. She passed it to me through the open window, but didn't open the door.

'What is it, Roberta?' she asked through the window.

'Just shoes, Mum. I know what it is.'

'Open it,' she ordered me.

I opened the parcel and the boots fell out onto the floor. Mum then opened the door and got in.

Until then I hadn't realised how afraid for me Mum was, and I felt very sorry for the anxiety my activities caused her. She was already an old woman, approaching seventy, having had me when she was forty. I couldn't stop doing what I was doing, though, not even to bring her peace. A better future for my children depended on what we were doing now, and if I lost my life in the process, I thought, far better to die for something I believed in than to have to live with regret for not struggling against the forces of racism and evil.

When two weeks were up, I left to attend the conference. The media coverage had alerted the police to the death threats, and although they scoffed they were obliged to extend some degree of protection towards participants, and the conference proceeded without incident.

7

I was at home in the flat in Sydney when I received a unexpected phone call from Ian in Melbourne. Some woman, he said, visiting from overseas had spoken to Leon Fink, saying she had heard that one of the Black leaders was a woman, and she wanted to meet her. The international media had carried news of the Embassy around the world, and we knew that pictures had made the front page of newspapers in countries as far away as Germany and the United States. This woman, Ian told me, was an Australian living in England, but she maintained an interest in what was happening here. She was in Australia to promote her book, The Female Eunuch. Had I heard of her? Germaine Greer?

The truth was that I could barely afford to eat, much less buy newspapers or magazines, and I didn't own a television. I tried to stay abreast of what was happening outside the Black community but as I was travelling around so much, well, no, I didn't know of this woman.

Leon wanted to introduce Germaine to me by phone

and, after I had spoken to her, I might agree to meet with her.

The accent of the woman who came on the line was a cross between British and Australian, but she was pleasant so I agreed to see her. We arranged to meet at the Jungle Bar at the top of the escalator at Wynyard Station. I didn't know this person and I felt that having a drink together would give us enough time for a first meeting. If I could see any purpose in it, perhaps I would meet her again.

I went to the local newsagent to see if I could find out who this woman was and, sure enough, dailies and magazines were all carrying news of her visit. She was being trumpeted as Australia's leading feminist who had made a big mark on the world stage, back home, amongst other things, to give a speech at Sydney Town Hall.

On learning this I became apprehensive about meeting her. What did she want with me? I phoned Gordon Briscoe, who was considered more an Aboriginal moderate than a militant, and asked him if he would accompany me. At least he knew who Germaine was, which was a real plus.

At this first meeting, Germaine did not come across as either high-powered or flamboyant which, for some reason, I had imagined she would. Later, when I knew her a little better, I considered the possibility that she had just been subdued until she could fathom my expectations.

Germaine asked a lot of questions about Kooris she had heard of through the news, most of them men. However, perhaps because she hadn't read anything about Gordon, she only made light conversation with him. Then again, she may have thought Gordon and I were an item, or that he was my bodyguard, neither of which was the case.

Her interest in our community programs pleased me, and we met several times, whenever I was up from Canberra. Once, Paul Coe and I were guests on the television program 'Monday Conference', and Germaine phoned me at the studio. I told her I was flying back immediately but, as it turned out, I missed the last plane to Canberra, so Robert Moore, the program's host, invited Paul and me back to his home for dinner. Germaine learned of this and phoned me again at his flat, inviting me to join her at a party, and Paul had no intention of being left out.

The party was held at a grand mansion in Centennial Park, and the guests included Leon and Margaret Fink, Gordon Barton, and numerous other luminaries, most of whom, of course, I did not know. While Germaine and I stood by the huge columns at the front of the house, she loudly gave me a running commentary on every man who walked past alone. She was sending up the way in which men often spoke about women, discussing their physical features and attributing behaviours to them on that basis. 'That's one a fat slob, just look at his gut. Oh, now he's got a cute butt, I bet he can go. Hmm, and that one, he's very nice looking—but I hear he's the town bike.' She had me in fits of laughter, while the men, red-faced and disbelieving her audacity, didn't know how to react.

Paul tried to work the crowd inside, but it appeared to me from the distance that people were in a party mood and not open to his attempts to inform them of Aboriginal politics. Eventually he joined Germaine and me, and he elaborated on a feed-the-children program he was involved in, which I had mentioned to her earlier. The aim of the project was to prepare breakfast for inner-city children before school and it was operating with the assistance and under the largesse of the Wayside Chapel in Kings Cross. Germaine was very interested and wished to see the program in action, so we told her she would have to be up very early next day in order to do so. Then we took our leave.

The next morning we must have been a curious sight as we made our way through Surry Hills towards the park where the program was operating in Darlington. Despite the cold, Germaine wore high-heel sandals and with her long legs she fairly bounded along. I had to really pump my legs and run to keep up with her.

When we'd inspected the program, Germaine said she would see what she could do to round up support. This came to fruition some time later when I was contacted by her friend, Leon Fink.

At one of our meetings I mentioned to Germaine that I intended going to Alice Springs, and she asked if she could accompany me. I laughed, because at that stage I had no idea how I was going to get there, and couldn't imagine her trying to hitch a lift alongside me. When she heard this she said she would pay the expenses if she could come along. We could fly, although she'd prefer to go by car; it would be more exciting and we'd see more. Did I drive? she asked me, because she did not.

I was surprised by the apparent contradiction of Germaine, an independent feminist, who was dependent on someone to drive her around.

Eventually Germaine said she had pulled a plan together: a friend of hers would lend us a car.

Before we left I laid down some basic rules including no cameras. I wanted the Aboriginal people in the

Centre to accept me, and I didn't want anyone travelling with me to be in a position to exploit them. I planned to camp in the Todd River creekbed and realised that other folk camped there would have little privacy and therefore be open to exploitation on film. I also did not want to be followed. If I walked up and spoke to anyone, I said, Germaine was not to come over to join me unless I indicated it was okay to do so. I knew Germaine did not know much about traditional Aboriginal etiquette, such as the need to cast your eyes down and not eye-ball people, at least until they felt comfortable in your presence and sometimes not at all. Germaine's piercing scrutiny, I had read, was enough to unnerve all manner of high-fliers overseas. What traditional Aboriginal people would make of her, I had no idea.

When we met to pick up the car, I was carrying only a small amount of gear and I encouraged Germaine to do likewise. She hoped I didn't mind, she said, but she had packed a polaroid camera. She thought people we met might like to have a photograph of themselves. As she planned to give them the photos, I agreed.

Her friend, whom she introduced to me as 'Peter', was messing around with the car, a Valiant station wagon, when we arrived at his place. He was a burly man, big and pudgy. He was stacking things in the car—a mattress, a bag—as if he were coming too, so I asked Germaine. 'Umm,' she said, 'well, yes.' At the last moment he had said he wanted to come and she thought he would withdraw the loan of his car if she refused.

I was uneasy but Germaine said she had things under control. At least there was someone to share the driving on this long journey and if the trip turned sour because of his company, we'd just leave him and continue some other way.

We were barely out of Sydney when we had our first taste of disaster, a retread stripped off the tyre. When I saw this I was outraged. Fancy setting off to drive two thousands miles through one of the most sparsely populated deserts on earth—on retreads! Peter changed the tyre and we continued a little way before another retread stripped off another tyre.

Germaine knew nothing about cars or desert travel. I had cut my teeth on both with trips around Mt Isa, Townsville and Brisbane, and polished my experience during the trip to Perth. As well, I was quite mechanically minded, having messed around a bit with cars and motorbikes during my youth.

We had to limp to the next garage where we had new tyres fitted all round, I suspect at Germaine's expense. From there on the trip was, mechanically at least, largely uneventful.

Our journey was well underway when I discovered Peter had a case full of camera equipment stowed under a cloth in the rear. I was very angry and sought to extract from him the same promise as I had from Germaine. He was too casual in his replies and agreement, so I knew I'd have to watch him. He didn't strike me as a particularly ethical type, a fact I would have known if I'd had the opportunity to do some research on him before we'd left.

Germaine was an excellent travel companion, taking upon herself the task of staying awake and chatting with whoever was driving. From her conversation I realised she was having an affair with Michael Willesee, who at the time was a top television presenter. His sister, Geraldine, a journalist, was a committed supporter of our struggle. Much of Germaine's conversation disturbed me, including the degree of intimacy she seemed happy to share, such as 'a blood-stained handprint on the bonnet of the car' being her fond memory of one of their encounters. As compensation for her inability to drive, Germaine took over as much as she could in other ways. When we stopped at a garage for showers, for instance, she insisted I have first shower and I found she had washed my dusty clothes in the handbasin by the time I'd finished.

We travelled to Adelaide, then Port Augusta and on up, through the night, to Coober Pedy. At one stage I was catching some rest on a mattress in the back as we rocked around on the sandy track which constituted the road, and when I woke up we had another person in the car. His semitrailer had broken down, I was told, and we were giving him a lift. He had promised to show us where we could buy petrol at any hour in Coober Pedy.

The harder sleeping conditions are, the deeper I seem to sleep. When I next woke we were in Coober Pedy, outside some sort of underground nightclub. As Peter refilled the tank, Germaine leaned against the rear window, effectively stopping anyone from looking into the car and spotting me in the darkness.

When we left, Germaine told me that a man had come out of the club and approached her, asking if she was interested in having a man. He had many clean friends, he said, she could have as many as she liked. They had money and opals. Germaine listened to him in amazement and said, 'If you think I've driven two thousand miles for a fuck, you can forget it.'

I laughed. Germaine, at six foot two, is, to many men, distinctly unapproachable. The man had a lot of gall, but absolutely no luck. He'd chosen to sexually proposition one of the world's leading feminists. Dumb move. Damned dumb move!

Germaine began having second thoughts about camping in the creekbed. Couldn't we just spend all day there then sneak back and sleep in a motel late at night? She fancied having a shower. 'How can we learn the hardships faced by the people who have to live in the creekbed all the time?' I countered.

Germaine also wanted to have a go at driving. Twin ruts in the sand ran to the horizon in both directions, not another car on the road, not a tree in sight, but she still almost killed us all. She picked up speed, then lost control so that the car began to bounce sideways, back and forwards on each side of the deep ruts. We hit a shallower patch in the road and the car lurched off across the desert. We all agreed this wasn't the place for her to learn.

Peter was a complete pain in the neck, to Germaine much more than to me. His manners and ignorance were appalling, he was uncouth and interrupted any conversation that Germaine and I began. But worse, he declared his love for Germaine, which he then thought gave him licence to carry on like a fool. Even halfway through the trip, when we stopped to eat, Germaine and I would order our meal then go and stand in the ladies' room to avoid his company while our food was being prepared.

By the time we arrived in Alice Springs, the Valiant was in a bad way and had to be booked in for a service and repair. The garage loaned us a vehicle to use while this was being done. It was a big American car, an unconverted left-hand drive, which meant the driver had to be virtually in the gutter while driving along.

I had done a bit of homework and had the address

of an Aboriginal woman, Joyce Clague, and her husband, Colin, who, I'd been told, would be pleased to see us and give us assistance. Although Joyce hailed from Bundjalung country on the east coast, she had very good relationships with a large number of traditional people.

Joyce offered us showers, refreshments and advice on the local scene, and did not appear surprised when I told her we intended to camp in the creekbed. While Joyce and I talked, Germaine again hand-washed my clothes, and because Peter was lounging around talking to her, he dumped his dirty clothes in the tub too. He then produced a camera and took a photo of her scrubbing over the wash-tub which, to my amazement and disgust, he later sold to a Sydney newspaper which ran it on the front page. Of course by that time, all the washing Germaine was doing was 'his', and the liberated woman was made to appear domestically shackled.

After a quick trip to the supermarket to pick up basic supplies, we drove to the creekbed, threw the mattresses on the ground and set up our camp. We were exhausted from the trip, and with the melancholy sounds of a distant didgeridu playing in our ears, we fell into a sound sleep.

When I began to stir next morning, I could hear Germaine fiddling around with some things on her side of the double mattress which we shared. When I opened my eyes, Germaine presented me with a tin of apricots, the lid removed and a spoon upright in it, and said, 'Room service!' in a very Hollywood manner. I had to laugh.

However, we soon learned some of the many discomforts of camping in the creekbed, lack of toilet facilities being one of them. Later, we spoke with other camping families and groups, all Aboriginal, and they asked us if we had heard a car during the night. Some white yobbos, knowing Aboriginal families were living in their path, had driven a vehicle quickly along the middle of the creekbed, and parents had been lucky to snatch their sleeping children out of its way. We had placed our camp very much to the side, and I doubt that the sound of a herd of elephants would have woken me, such was my tiredness.

One shy woman, sitting on a blanket with an infant in her lap, hissed for my attention as Germaine and I walked away. When I returned, alone, she pulled a rather ragged-edged magazine out from under the blanket, flicked it open to a page, and said to me, 'Is that her? That white woman?' I looked and saw a photo of Germaine, and when I nodded, her eyes opened wide with pleasure and surprise, and we both laughed.

Germaine could only spend a short time in Alice as she had to fly back to give her speech at the Sydney Town Hall. We used the time as best we could, talking to people and, one day, attending a session at the court house. When we arrived I was pleased to see a lot of Aboriginal people just standing around in the courtroom. One of the things we were advocating in Sydney was that Blacks, particularly youths, should go into courts and familiarise themselves with the environment and proceedings so that, should they later be arrested, they might not be so intimidated by the process. I was disturbed then to learn that all the Aboriginal people standing around so casually were up on charges.

Taking a seat at the press table, I thought I'd write a story on the day for *Nation Review*. (*The Review* became *Nation Review* in 1972.) I was immediately challenged. As

I didn't carry press papers I had to vacate the chair. I moved to one of the long benches directly behind the table and pulled out my notebook and pencil. The courtroom attendant came over again straightaway to tell me I was not permitted to write in the court. I said, 'I understand I'm allowed to do anything in the court as long as I don't make noise. Isn't that right?' Germaine took a seat towards the back.

Not long after proceedings began, a local reporter came in and sat at the press table. After he had taken out his notebook and pen, he turned to look at me making notes with my pad balanced on my lap. 'Come and sit up here,' he said. 'These seats are all empty. I'm the only one who ever comes here, except when there's a big case, a murder trial or something.' With his permission, I joined him.

By the time court recessed, we had begun to discern a pattern to the magistrate's sentencing. The overwhelming majority of charges against Aborigines, men and women, were for 'drunk and disorderly'. The couple of white defendants were heard first, on more serious charges, and their cases held over to be scheduled for another day. Then the long procession of Aboriginal people began shuffling into the dock.

'Drunk and disorderly, Your Honour,' the prosecutor intoned as each new face took the stand.

'How do you plead?' The magistrate barely glanced at the defendant, his eyes scanning the papers in front of him.

Mumble, mumble, came each Aborigine's reply, at which there was a pause, and the magistrate would then calculate the person's punishment. His system seemed to operate on this basis: if the person had not been arrested at all since the beginning of the year, he or she was cautioned and discharged. Those who had been arrested previously were fined. The penalties rose in increments of ten dollars for each offence. It was obvious from the poverty of their clothes and their demeanour that hardly anyone could make their fine, so they were actually being sent to gaol for similarly incremental periods stated by the magistrate. Each person's case took only a few minutes to be heard, none had legal representation, and most had very little grasp of English. It was an assembly line of Black people being tossed into gaol.

Only one, a young woman, said 'not guilty', at which the magistrate's head snapped up. He made her repeat the plea, it seemed that he thought he had misheard it.

'Go to the back of the court. I'll hear you later,' he said, and she quietly padded on her bare feet to wait at the end of the queue.

Close to a hundred people were being heard in the court that day, a goodly number of whom had already been processed by the time the magistrate announced recess. Everyone crowded onto the verandah for a breath of fresh air.

I sat on a long bench outside where 'prisoners' and spectators alike were mingling, close by some very young Aboriginal girls. After pausing a moment to speak with the young woman who had pled not guilty, Germaine joined me. I had by then struck up a conversation with the young girl sitting nearest me, who was very dark and pretty and spoke English quite well.

As soon as Germaine sat down, she leaned across me and asked the girl, 'Were you in the lock-up on the weekend?' at which the girl nodded. 'Do the police ever hit you?' The girl looked around to ensure that she was not going to be overheard, and replied quietly, 'Yes.'

'Do they try to have sex with you?' Germaine continued, and the girl, blushing and squirming on her seat,
again answered affirmatively.

'How many times? How many times have police had
sex with you?' A tone of outrage had entered Germaine's voice, and even she was looking around to
make sure no one was eavesdropping.

'Five or six times,' the young girl replied.

'Five or six times?' Germaine was agitated and indig-
nant. 'Five or six times *when*?'

'Five or six times—last night,' was the girl's quiet
reply. Germaine leapt to her feet and walked to the
edge of the verandah. I could see that the girl thought
perhaps she had said something wrong to upset Germaine, so I took her thin hand in mine and, gently
stroking it, said, 'It's alright. Nothing's the matter. She
just wanted to know, that's all.'

By the time court was reconvened, the magistrate
had been made aware of the presence of Germaine in
the room. Every case which he then heard, he cautioned and discharged, breaking the pattern he had
established earlier.

By lunch break we had seen and heard enough, and
decided to spend the afternoon doing something else.
The young woman who Germaine had spoken to had
told her that she had pleaded 'not guilty' because she
had a baby at home and she wasn't going to go to gaol
'this time'.

That night in a restaurant, when Germaine and I took
up our usual place in the ladies' room while waiting for
our meal, we discussed the events of the day. Germaine
appeared to be devastated and talked at length of the
young girl's apparent lack of indignation at her situation. 'It's probably happened to her older sisters and

her friends, and maybe she just thinks it's her turn now. Rape must be a way of life out here,' she said. I agreed that this might be true, but added that, even if this were the case, the girl would still suffer enormous loss of self-esteem. 'It will be a wonder,' I added, 'if she doesn't turn out alcoholic. It's a major problem out here.'

We were continuing to discuss the impact of rape on the psyche when Germaine suddenly stared me in the eyes and said, 'You know so much about this. Have *you* been raped?'

'Yes,' I replied, 'but I don't talk about it,' and demurred from giving details. I did not then know that I would come to deeply regret my own honesty.

8

I had been apprehensive about Germaine's departure from Alice Springs, wondering how I would return to Sydney. I didn't have any cash to pay for a flight, and I certainly didn't fancy travelling alone with Peter. He solved my dilemma by announcing that he was flying back with Germaine, and leaving me to drive his car back alone. He said he'd cover the expenses.

The trip was hazardous. Instead of returning through Adelaide, I chose to go up the highway, then right to Mt Isa and out onto the coast. A longer route, but more populated. I was pursued for miles up the highway by menacing drinkers in Tennant Creek after I had stopped there briefly at a hotel–petrol pump to take on fuel. Later, a front tyre blew out when I was travelling at over a hundred miles an hour. Fortunately there wasn't another car within sight nor a tree within cooee, and I was able to wrestle the steering wheel to a safe stop. A series of flash storms hit once I passed the Isa, turning the dirt roads into a thick grey mud. Along with other drivers and their passengers, I helped us all to cross a flooded river, and then, just as night fell, another storm hit and we all became bogged.

In the morning we trudged for miles overland, in the direction that one of our number claimed to have seen the lights of a town the previous night. The thick mud stuck to our legs and forced us to pause every few yards to scrape some off with sticks. Otherwise, with the weight of it, we would not have been able to continue.

We spent five or six days in that little town, which was just a railway siding consisting only of a hotel, church Hall and a few houses. The hotel was unable to accommodate everyone and most of the men from the group had to camp in the Hall. When the ground became sufficiently firm again, an earth-moving company offered to bring the cars in so we could put them on a train and freight them to Cloncurry where the bitumen road to the coast began. From there, I travelled on to Townsville, where I took the opportunity to pay a very brief visit to my children, then on through Brisbane, where I picked up a passenger, Sammy Watson Junior, who was a regular at the Embassy, and on to Sydney where I left the car before continuing to Canberra.

I was happy to tell my Embassy colleagues about the interest in our activities which I had assessed on my wide travels. Many Aborigines in the Centre had heard of the Embassy though few knew the rationale behind it. My task had been to explain as well as I could what we were hoping to achieve.

On my return to Sydney I began asking questions about Peter, whose surname I had learned was Carette. He had not spent all his time in Alice Springs with Germaine and me, and I was worried that he may have taken inappropriate or culturally offensive photos, perhaps even using the zoom lenses I had seen in his box. I was dismayed to learn that he was the photographer who had donned a medical smock and, posing as a doctor, sneaked into Marianne Faithful's hospital room and photographed her as she lay unconscious from a suspected drug overdose while in Australia with Mick Jagger. I felt that Germaine must have been aware of his history when she'd made her arrangements with him, and I was alarmed that perhaps I had, once more, naively trusted someone with something so important and been let down. Would I never learn?

A support group in New Zealand invited me to tour their country and spread word of our activities. In addition to our protest group at the Embassy, we now also had a rather clandestine inner circle, called the National Black Caucus. The Caucus was planning protest marches to be held in all capital cities throughout Australia on National Aborigines' Day, the second Friday in July, and we were calling for international support.

I was apprehensive about the reception I might receive from my sister, Della, who had rejected the racism of Australia and gone to live in New Zealand. So I wrote advising her of my visit and leaving it up to her to decide whether she wanted to associate herself with me, and therefore possibly with the movement I was now seen to represent. I need not have worried. She was at the airport to greet me and organised as much time as possible to spend with me. Unbeknown to me, Della attended a public meeting at which I was the guest speaker, and later teased me with, 'All my life I've had to listen to you, and now I find I'm even happy to *pay* to listen to you.'

Della had prospered in New Zealand, having scored a good job using her administrative skills with a firm of accountants. With her quick mind and organising abilities, she had risen in the company to become supervisor of her area and, with additional training, was very well placed for advancement into the highly technical sphere of computer progamming. I was pleased for her, and sorry and humiliated that Australia had not yet seen fit to offer similar opportunities to Black women.

This was my first trip outside Australia and it made an enormous impact on me. I learned during my travels that Maori and South Sea Island people represented more than ninety per cent of prisoners in maximum security, had abysmally low education and employment rates and many lived in extreme poverty. However, my first sight in New Zealand was of a brown-skinned uniformed man leaving from the cockpit of the plane in which I had arrived. A pilot, co-pilot or navigator for the airline, he was the first person of colour I had ever seen working in this capacity and it took my breath away. Despite feeling that people of colour could do everything anyone else can do, in Australia I had been deprived of any opportunity to actually *see* this, and perhaps doubts instilled by the racism of my earlier experiences lingered. Otherwise I am at a loss to explain the pleasure and shock I received to see this man alight from the plane!

Driving around Auckland I saw Maori women working in food shops, cutting and handling sandwiches for their white customers. This, too, was something I had never seen before, and to this day it is still a rare sight in Australia.

During my brief stay I met many wonderful Maori people, including a special couple, Syd and Hana Jackson, who made my trip magic by sharing a great deal of Maori culture with me. Now divorced, Hana remains my dear friend and regular correspondent. I also met with the Polynesian Panthers, and was so taken by the earnest commitment of one of the organisers, Will Ilolahea, that on my return I suggested he be invited to Australia to look around and attend our National Aborigines' Day march.

Germaine had preceded me to New Zealand and been arrested for using obscene language. I suffered no such fate as my ideology did not stretch to these types of freedoms. My talks and television appearance focused on the one thing I considered obscene, the way that I and other Black people were being treated in Australia, and I was able to present factual and statistical data which supported this idea.

Soon after I returned to Sydney Denis Walker rang me from Brisbane—an emergency. A young Murri woman, who I shall refer to here only as A, was in trouble. Would I take her in?

After being raped when she was fifteen and sixteen years old, now aged seventeen she had again been recently raped by a businessman while hitching from her home town to Brisbane. She went directly to a hospital for medical assistance and tests, and then to a police station to file a complaint. At the police station, she became distressed by the offensive way the officers were speaking to her, and when she responded in kind they threw her onto the floor and pulled her coat up over her head to subdue her. They then charged her with indecent language and put her in a cell.

When Denis learned of A's whereabouts he went to the station and bailed her out. She had given police the car licence plate number of the offender and the case would have seemed, on the surface, to be quite straightforward. However, instead of arresting the perpetrator, police began a search for A, officiously visiting houses where they thought she might be staying. The manner in which they did this so upset people that they felt there was a real risk to A's life. Hence Denis' call. They wanted to smuggle her out of Queensland to a safe house.

A was distraught when she arrived, and after I spoke to her I realised she was also suicidal. Her self-esteem was at an all-time low, she was stressed about her situation and desperately unhappy about having to leave her home and friends under these circumstances. As she became increasingly depressed I decided that a complete change of environment was required, she needed to go somewhere where she could feel safe and be in relaxed and caring company. I contacted my Maori friend, Hana, and asked if she and Syd would take A in if I could get her to New Zealand. Hana agreed.

A's predicament later became the subject of a pamphlet put out by a Canberra-based coalition, Joint Women's Action and the Black Liberation Front, and was further discussed in the press. Her life has moved on far past these events and it would compound the tragedy to revisit them upon her now.

A was just one of many Black rape victims I met during that time. The majority had not even contacted the police because they'd anticipated the reception they would receive. That A was an active member of the Black struggle for liberation had heightened her awareness and caused her to think she had a 'right' to protection by the police under the law. The fact that, in claiming this right, she had been forced to go into voluntary exile was pitiful and an indictment on police action and Australian social mores.

Not long after this, the Australian Union of Students organised an information and support-seeking trip for me to Papua New Guinea, with visits planned to Rabaul, Lae and Port Moresby. In Rabaul, in the company of Mataungan Association leader John Kaputin, who later became a politician when Papua New Guinea was granted independence, and his parents and clan, I committed my first major international faux pax. At the beginning of a special lunch prepared in my honour, I was presented with a very large egg which had been simmered in coconut milk. Eggs were one of the foods I had eliminated from my diet as a means to avoid asthma and stomach upset, as I have an allergy to albumen. So I declined to accept it, although I noticed that no one else had been given one. John quietly tried to insist that I should eat it, but I was adamant. I was scheduled to speak to a large meeting that afternoon and couldn't afford to risk not being at my best.

Across the bay from Rabaul sits a huge volcanic mountain, and in the warm ashes near the top a local bird lays its eggs and leaves them to hatch. Eggs laid too high are exposed to excessive heat and perish. These are the only eggs that can be removed. When a special guest is to be feted, youths from John's village race each other across these shark-infested waters and up the mountainside to where their feet begin to burn in the ash. The first youth to locate an egg by delving around with their hand in the heat holds the prize aloft, and it is carried home and served to the honoured guest. If only I had known!

The afternoon presentation turned out to be almost the largest, and certainly the most varied, assembly I have ever had the privilege of addressing. Representatives from three language groups attended, and each was provided with an interpreter who shared the platform with me, translating each sentence as it was spoken. A long and somewhat unwieldy process, the audience sat transfixed through more than five hours of talk. John expressed great satisfaction at the end. He told me it was the first Mataungan Association meeting that women had attended, and some of the people had walked through dense jungle for two days to be there. They had heard that 'a woman warrior' was going to speak and had made it their business not to miss me. I was humbled by their attention and flattered with their response. When the meeting broke up, the crowd surged forward to touch me. Elders, wearing local attire and adorned with feathers, paint, shell-money ropes around their necks and bones pierced through their skins, came up to shake my hands. One delved into his straw dilly-bag and rattled around, pulling out his only coin, a sixpence, which he extended to me to take to my people. I cannot adequately express the great pleasure this meeting gave me. It made all my work and the hardships I had been through feel worthwhile.

In Lae I met Michael Somare, soon to become that country's first prime minister. He seemed concerned that if he was seen to support my mission it may put him off-side with the Australian authorities who were then running his country. In Port Moresby, university students, artists and writers, including renowned poet John Kasaipwalova from the Tobriand Islands, organised my presentations and promised to support our struggle.

On returning to Sydney Gary Williams and I, as key organisers for the forthcoming National Aborigines'

ROBERTA SYKES

Day march, were summoned to Police Headquarters in Surry Hills. We were sat down in a room full of hefty white men—detectives—and told not to be nervous! I responded that I had more reason to be nervous than Gary, being the only female in the room. Everyone laughed, which broke the ice, and the police proceeded to question us politely about the route we planned to take and the number of people we thought would attend. The size of turnout, they said, would determine whether the police should halt traffic in the area so we could walk on the streets. Detective Fred Longbottom introduced himself as being in charge of the operation.

As well, we had made a formal approach to the Town Hall as we wished to use the steps of the Town Hall, in the centre of George Street, as the platform for the speeches. Although many other demonstrations had been granted this leeway, we were told to use the back steps instead. Organisers became incensed by this rejection, interpreting it to mean that Blacks were, as usual, required to use the back door, to take the seat at the back of the bus. We could barely believe their insensitivity.

When the day dawned, thousands of people turned up in Sydney. A large truck with a cage structure built into its back platform had been converted into a travelling kindergarten in which Koori children played as they participated. Transport had been provided to bring people in from La Perouse and other outlying suburbs.

Unfortunately, despite our efforts to involve Aboriginal Elders and people who the police should have realised were quite moderate, uniformed officers seemed to anticipate trouble. Without provocation, they moved in to arrest some Black men, Will Ilolahea, visiting from New Zealand, amongst them. These actions angered the crowd and when we reached the Town Hall, we defied the authorities by setting up out the front. Some unionists began to urge the crowd to storm the steps, which were being guarded by a solid line of police.

I could see alarm rising on the faces of many of the Black women and Elders in the crowd; they had come out to this—for many, their first demonstration—on the understanding that no one would provoke trouble or violence. So, I took the microphone and called for peace. Our union brothers, I said, were running ahead of us, and I called on them to remember that this was a Black demonstration and that they shouldn't try to take our leadership away from us by trying to make people go in a direction they did not want to take. I was thoroughly and roundly applauded, and the afternoon newspaper labelled me a 'Peacemaker'. This was one of the few caps created for me by the media that I was not unhappy to wear.

Towards the end of the presentations, a message came to us up on the speakers' platform that another of our number had been surreptitiously arrested. Gary Foley took the microphone and scattered expletives through his short address. Immediately I noticed the dismay of some the Elders and also that several officers had begun champing at the bit to arrest him. So I again took the microphone and said, 'Well, Gary should not have said ****. But it's a fact that a lot of innocent people have been arrested just for attending this march.' We took up a collection to try to raise bail.

As the crowd began to disperse, we noticed the police surging forward to nab Gary. Since I had used the same word, I suggested Gary stand towards the back of the underground railway entrance that we were using for a platform and I stood out on the edge, thinking they might arrest me instead. Given the overwhelming reception I had been given earlier by the crowd, arresting me would prove a very unpopular exercise and I was interested to see how the police would react. Instead, some police doubled around the back of the platform and grabbed Gary by the legs. Supporters on the platform grabbed his shoulders, and when I turned around I could see a tug of war going on, with slightly built Gary in danger of being torn in two.

Quite suddenly, he wasn't there. I asked, 'Where's Gary?'

'Oh,' said a Koori wag, quick as lightning, 'we got him off the police and dropped him over the back into Town Hall station. He was last seen doing a hundred miles an hour in the station, and when a train came through doing only eighty miles, he slowed down and jumped on it!' Talk about humour—there are some Blacks who can find something funny to say about almost everything.

I confronted Detective Longbottom, whose face I had seen in the crowd. 'Why did you try to arrest Foley?' I asked.

'He swore.'

'So did I!'

'I didn't hear you swear,' he replied.

'I said ****,' I persisted.

'But I didn't hear you,' he said, patronisingly ignoring me and gazing up at the front of the Town Hall.

'I said ****, ****, ****,' I continued until I regained his attention.

Shaking his forefinger at me, he said, 'Ah, but I'd proceed against you by summons, *if* I had heard you,' and then smirked and walked away.

My reason for confronting the detectives, quite apart from the occurrence on that day, was because many of our key organisers were being constantly arrested on obscene language charges by police who used obscene language themselves in the process of the arrest. The result was that many organisers were almost afraid to come out of hiding for fear of being imprisoned for unpaid fines emanating from these petty and hypocritical charges. I also hoped to publicly highlight how selectively these charges were being brought, even amongst Black organisers.

We were saddened that thirteen people had been arrested at our march, but heartened when the news came in that rallies had also taken place in Newcastle, Brisbane, Melbourne and Canberra. In Port Moresby, students had taken to the streets. In Lae, students had taken custody of an Australian Government representative who refused to pass on their message of protest to the Australian Government. When they set him free, he left the area when told that his safety could no longer be guaranteed. A rally was also held outside Australia House in London.

As Canberra's winter had deepened and our Embassy had continued to function, we'd begun to hear rumours that the government planned to change the law in order to move us. We had heard similar rumours in the past, but some politicians had thought that when conditions became freezing, we would pack up our tents and go. How wrong they were! The additional hardship served to strengthen our resolve, especially when we compared our camp, in the middle of the nation's capital and in full sight of the public eye, to the makeshift accommodation and harsh conditions that were permanently 'home' to the majority of Aborigines right across the country. We felt we couldn't complain.

Rumours of our imminent removal began to intensify. We had a variety of people in high places who channelled information to us, many of whom were unwilling to publicly identify themselves with our mission.

A group of us were, as often happened, holding a planning meeting in Sydney when someone informed us that word had come in that the Embassy would be torn down and its residents evicted shortly after dawn the next day. Our informant had even sent several plane tickets to enable key people to fly in on the first plane. Gary Foley and I were amongst those elected by the group to go.

When we arrived, early on the bright sunny though cold morning of Thursday, 20 July 1972, we found the Embassy residents already up, dressed and sitting around drinking cups of tea. They too had learned that Ralph Hunt, Minister for the Interior, had gazetted a Bill in the early hours of that morning to clear the way for our Embassy to be closed down. As we waited, more supporters began to arrive, Faith Bandler amongst them, as well as a small posse of reporters with cameras. We didn't have too long to wait before a fleet of police cars and wagons hove into view.

What followed was bedlam. We'd formed a circle, linking arms, around the Embassy's central tent, singing 'We Shall Not Be Moved' and watched as police tore down all the other tents and threw away people's personal belongings. We were then ordered to stand aside, and when we refused to do so, we were attacked.

Although we tried to resist, we had to disperse under their brutal assault and I ran onto the street to get photographs of what was happening. Police had earlier blocked off the road so there wasn't any danger from vehicles. I was pursued by police while taking photos and carried off, photographed by an officer and put into the wagon. In the process, the police arresting me managed to ensure that my legs were drawn over the sharp edge of a step up into the vehicle, scraping all the skin off my shins. I cried out with the sharp pain, and others already in the wagon caught me and helped me up. Even more joined us, some being thrown in so roughly that they fell onto the floor and hit and injured their heads on the wagon's tough floor. The two Garys, Foley and Williams, were amongst those of us who had been arrested.

At Canberra Police Station, we were unloaded into a large cage in the basement. I was the only woman present. We were made to stand apart from each other under the eye of an officer who stood by the door. I was concerned when, one by one, the men were taken upstairs to be formally charged and it appeared that I was going to be left alone in the cage with just a male officer. When I voiced my fears a Koori man was left with me until a female officer, who was off-duty and had to be called in, at last arrived.

The officer in the cage had told me that I was to be charged with 'about twelve' counts of assaulting police, and that they had video-tape evidence to support these charges. When the time came, however, I was charged with obstructing traffic. I was less than charmed by the police woman's description of my hair typed on the charge form. 'Frizzy,' she wrote. 'Haven't you ever heard of an afro?' I inquired.

With Eric Strasser's help I was eventually released on my own recognisance and approached by television scouts to appear on Michael Willesee's show, 'A Current Affair'. I was to fly to Sydney and be interviewed, by co-axial cable, by Michael in Melbourne. I already had a return ticket but I used the ticket they gave me to take Gary Williams with me. We were both sore and badly bruised as we were brought to the studio.

Gary was an articulate young man with a great deal of potential whose risks that day had been the same as my own, and so I was highly suspicious of why I'd been singled out to appear on the show. I was asked to stand by a curtain and come out on-camera when I heard my name called. Gary stood by me. When I heard my name I gave Gary a push and he went out and did the program in my stead. I watched him on a little monitor and, replete with dust and bruises of the day, he gave viewers a clear picture of the events we had endured.

Over the next three days we were busy organising. We planned to re-erect the Embassy on Parliament's front lawn on Sunday. Bus loads of people were being brought in for support.

Some of us were in Canberra on Saturday to finalise arrangements. We were informed that Ralph Hunt had sent a telegram to Alice Springs, cancelling an appointment he had there and saying he had to stay on in Canberra because he was expecting 'a blood-bath'. Up to this point we had managed well as we went about our preparations, but news of the cable injected great apprehension into our proceedings. A federal politician with insider-knowledge was predicting bloodshed, and we knew the blood was meant to be ours. Some of the organisers stayed up all night anxiously but, as usual when times are tough, I managed to sleep.

Commercial and public television cameras were in place on the day, and many of the events which transpired made the evening news. Hundred of armed police stormed across the lawns and beat up un-armed demonstrators, men and women alike, and several of our people were carried away by ambulance. We were told that a contingent of soldiers was standing at the ready, out of sight behind Parliament House, in case the efforts of the police force were not successful. I was a marshall that day, one of the first to be knocked out of the way, with the following lines of police then running over me. Cheryl Buchanan was struck on the spine and injured. Our Embassy tent was again removed.

Some media reports stated that several police officers had been injured and taken to hospital. A leak at the hospital provided us with reports on these injuries. They consisted in the main of abrasions to the hands, where knuckles had connected with people's faces and teeth.

The Aboriginal Embassy had been operating peacefully for seven months. We had carefully tended the lawn by constantly moving the tents around, and over time hundreds of tour buses had put us on their itineraries. We had been visited by state premiers, politicians and overseas visitors. Yet in full view of all these interested people and more, William McMahon's Liberal government had taken this violent action against us. With the stroke of a pen, it had made our protest 'illegal'. Members of the government were unaware of the extent to which this would eventually backfire on them.

Not to be easily defeated, we ventured to put up a new tent the following weekend. We found it impossible to believe that what was legal one day could have been made illegal the next. Our organisation was assisted by the media coverage our assault had received, and offers of assistance came in from right across Australia.

Coincidentally, the country was in the middle of a petrol strike, which made it difficult for everyone who wanted to support us to attend. Kooris who drove up in a bus from Victoria each had to contribute a small can of petrol to fill the tank.

Organisers were gratified when thousands responded to the call to attend. The Adelaide Aboriginal community sent a bus load of strong men, ready to be on the defensive if required. Sydney sent several buses, carrying not only Blacks but also union members who wished to support our efforts. A bus load of people from Brisbane arrived, and we had to find warmer clothing for many of them as they had not anticipated how cold it would be.

Unfortunately not everyone on the lawn that day was there with good intent. Marshalling once more, I walked past a group of bikies, one of whom flashed a knife and said, 'I'll get a piggie for you today, my lovely.' I was mortified! I knew that if anyone responded to the police violence with their own violence, we Blacks would get the blame.

My most poignant memory of that day, however, is of an elderly white couple who were sitting quietly holding hands on the grass. They were right in the way. I thought perhaps they didn't know what was going on, so I approached them. They almost looked liked they were praying. Yes, they said, they did know this was an Aboriginal protest, and that the police were likely to come. But they had seen the viciousness of the police on television the previous week, and if this is what Australia had come down to, they no longer wanted to live. They would be quite happy to sit there and let the police run over them and kill them, they said, such was their dismay and despair.

Prior to our demonstration, police came to the Students Union which we were using as our headquarters and requested a meeting with the leaders. They said they hoped to avoid the bloodshed of the previous week. We listened while they told us that it was their job to maintain law and order. Then we gave them our views on how they had turned an orderly protest into the melee which had come to reflect so poorly on them.

'But what can we do?' they asked. 'We've been set an impossible task.'

'Do you see all those buses that are arriving, bringing people in from all over the country?' I asked. 'Well, at the end of the day, what do you think those people will do? You have given the stipulation that you intend to remove the tents, if we put them up, at two o'clock. So, in fact, you've set the time for any clash that might occur. But what about three o'clock? What about four? And do you know that, at about five, most of the people have to get back on the buses and return to their homes in Sydney, Melbourne and elsewhere. Or did you think they were going to stay here?'

We could see the penny drop as expressions of understanding dawned on their faces. They had looked only at the removal of our Embassy as their imperative, not at the maintenance of law and order.

At two o'clock we stood at the ready around the tent we had erected. Nothing happened, no police came marching in columns across the street as they had a week earlier. By three, standing out in the warm sun, we were beginning, in fact, to get tired. At three-thirty, shadows were starting to lengthen in the short Canberra winter day, and some of the long distance buses were pulling in and loading up. Organisers and others sat in the tent Embassy, posing for pictures and collecting signatures for our records. Departing supporters felt triumphant because the tent remained erect so long past the police deadline. Our sheer numbers, it was felt, had staved off the attack.

The police, however, didn't want to be seen to have completely lost face, to have backed down, so as soon as the majority of protesters had left, a bunch of them came across the street and demanded the tent come down. We stood back and watched while they removed the pegs and uprights, rolled the canvas up and walked away. Quite a few of us were still there, and we whipped out another sheet of canvas and held it aloft with our hands. The tent, we felt, was not what was important, it was the symbolism of what it represented. A piece of ragged canvas held high by many hands still has the power to evoke that symbol of our destitution and living conditions, even today.

Police, by then on the other side of the street, looked over and saw what they mistook for another tent. They raced back, pounding their feet and pumping up their adrenalin. But when they got in very close, they saw that there was nothing there but our symbolic re-erection and, turning, they went off sheepishly. We followed them, laughing and chanting. One of our most bitter disappointments about the actions the police had taken against us was that, during the seven months through which our Embassy had stood, police had come by and often stopped to join us for hot tea or coffee, especially late on cold nights. They had chatted with us in a way which encouraged us to believe they were trying to be friendly, and it came as a harsh blow to have them then turn around and attack us when their political masters ordered them to do so. Our resentment at what we saw as their treachery found release in the taunts we hurled at them that day. Then we all packed up and left Canberra to return to our homes.

In Sydney, I was contacted by Leon Fink, and we met to talk about the needs of the feed-the-children program. Recent newspaper reports had said the program, which provided food for children on their way to school, was being well-attended but that the kids had to stand out in the rain and cold to eat because there wasn't any cover. Leon thought that he could help with this inadequacy and asked me to drive around with him to look at some empty buildings that might suit us. Only one was sufficiently central to be useful for the purpose: a disused warehouse in Shepherd Street, Chippendale, next door to a carpet factory.

I explained that we had absolutely no money to pay rent, and he said he was prepared to make the building available to us rent-free for a year. We would have to adapt the building to suit our needs. But we had no money to do that, either, so, with a sigh, he promised to see what he could do. We'd need, he said, a kitchen and cooking utensils, tiny tables and chairs, tiny toilets and wash-basins, but first the place would have to be cleaned out, lined and painted.

This all sounded like a dream to me as I looked around the dark interior of the building. I just couldn't envisage it coming true. Hopeful, yes. Optimistic, no. So I was greatly surprised as the project began to take shape, but I kept thinking the dream would disappear. While this was going on, Norma Ingram, Lyn Craigie and others were continuing to meet the needs of the children each morning, out in the cold in the park. I didn't dare share with them the news of the building because I thought that if it was suddenly withdrawn I would be the only one disappointed. Their task was so onerous that to burden them with a lift and then a let-down seemed to me to be incredibly unfair.

In a very short time Leon rang to tell me the build-ing was finished and that I could pick up the keys from him when he was next visiting the carpet factory which, as it turned out, he also owned. He gave me an inspec-tion and I had to pinch myself to make sure I was awake. As we looked around he said, 'Now, all you'll need will be plates and spoons and things.' He paused for a moment and, without my having said a word, he continued, 'Oh, alright. I'll give you the name of a com-pany. Go there and have them put it on my account.' I hastened to the address in Surry Hills and chose plain but serviceable dishes from the wholesaler Leon had nominated.

I still had the charge from my arrest in Canberra hanging over me. So, I made the rounds of some legal people I had met, several of whom offered to represent me for free, but I told them I wished to defend myself in court. All I required, I said, was advice. Paul Landa, later to become a NSW state politician, was amongst those who gave me their legal opinion on how to handle my defence. Eric Strasser, whom I normally turned to in legal matters, was not registered to prac-tise in Canberra, though following my arrest there he quickly took care of this oversight.

The case was looming, and though everyone said if I asked for a continuance I would get it, I had been invited to travel to England on a lecture tour and didn't wish to leave any matters unresolved here. I picked up the keys to the new quarters for the feed-the-children program the day before my departure for Canberra to have this case heard. Friends in Canberra had also asked me to accompany them to Thredbo for two days. I had never been to the snow and this prospect was attractive.

When I gave the keys to Lyn Craigie, I didn't have time to explain much at all. 'There's a warehouse in Chippendale that's been converted for you to use for the kids' breakfast program. You have it rent-free for a year. Here is the address, these are the keys. You can go over now and check it out. Sorry, I've got to run.' There was no disbelief on her face, just stunned surprise.

Four days later, when I returned from Canberra where I did not feel I had won my case even though it was 'proved but not recorded', I whizzed around the streets of Redfern and visited some of my usual haunts: the Legal Service and the Medical Service. While doing my rounds, I was surprised to hear rumours pertaining to my acquisition of the keys to the building. The benefactor was unknown at the time as I had omitted to mention his name in my hasty departure. Instead I found that the gift was being attributed to me, and there had been wild speculation about how I may have come by such a lot of money. Prostitution, it had been decided, seemed the only possible way.

I went storming off to Lyn Craigie's house in Burton Street, Darlinghurst. A recent police raid had seen her front door torn from its hinges so her place looked very patchy. Lyn was hanging her baby's nappies on the clothes line out the back and she warily invited me back there so that she could complete the task while her infant, Yeena, was sleeping. From her manner I knew that she realised I had heard the rumours and had worked out that she must have been party to their circulation, though I knew she hadn't come up with this stuff alone.

I followed Lyn up and down the clothes line, berating her, trying to get her to see sense. 'Gee, you must think I'm terrific. A prostitute who spends her money on children. Do you have any idea how much the building and renovations cost? A fortune! You must think I'm a terrific prostitute to have earned all that money. Or do you think maybe I just had one customer, someone who paid me a fortune for sex. Well, you must think I'm a terrific lay!'

Having said my piece, I didn't hang around. Lyn hadn't raised her eyes to me throughout the entire performance. I went back to my little flat in Surry Hills and sulked, giving my words time to get around. A day or two later, I went down to the building to check out what was happening. I found the women happily settling in, tidying up dishes, wiping counters, and absolutely thrilled about having the premises.

I took Lyn Craigie and Norma Ingram aside and said I wanted them to meet the owner. I had phoned Leon Fink and arranged a day when he would be spending time at the carpet factory, and got Lyn and Norma to agree to the time. With my trip to England pending, I knew I could no longer act the middle-man, they would have to deal with each other direct.

Although I'd blown up at Lyn, when I thought the whole thing through I wasn't even angry. A bit hurt, yes, but angry, no. None of us had had, up to this time, any experience with altruism. What few material goods we had we'd got by working, begging, borrowing and, sometimes, stealing. That someone would, out of the blue, give us something so valuable for nothing was completely beyond our experience. If I had doubted all along that we would actually end up with the use of the building, their reactions also had to be considered reasonable under the circumstances.

Norma and Lyn were charmed by Leon Fink, who told them that they were to call on him if there was anything more he could help them with. As a footnote to this episode, when I returned from England I again called by the Shepherd Street address. The place was operating wonderfully, upstairs had been turned into an administrative centre and new ideas for raising support for the centre and widening its field of operation had been generated. Norma pointed out to me that the upstairs section had been completely fitted out with new carpet.

'Oh,' I said, 'so who had to sleep with someone to get this?'

At this, we all had a good laugh.

The building later became the Murawina Preschool, which operated there for about eight years.

I had been invited to undertake a speaking tour in England by a group of expatriate Australians who called their organisation Abjab. The name, I was told, had no meaning. I was nervous about travelling so far to a country where I knew no one apart from the disembodied voice of a host on the phone, but quite apart from that, the notion of 'England' as the home base of the racism that flourished in Australia was not inviting.

When he realised how nervous I was, Michael Willesee, with whom I had become friendly through his relationship with Germaine, invited me out for a quick meal and a pep talk on the eve of my departure. He was a seasoned traveller through his television work, and on hearing that I had an overnight stopover in Singapore, told me to venture out of the hotel and go to Boogie Street to see something very unusual. He was encouraging and told me he had great faith in my ability to undertake an overseas lecture tour. I had my doubts.

Abjab organisers had decided they not only wanted a speaker, they also wanted someone who could write, which was why they had chosen me. Their invitation caused some jealousy and friction in certain sections of the Black community, and a telegram denouncing me as 'elitist and counter-revolutionary' was anonymously sent to the organisers. When this telegram was read to me over the phone I immediately recognised the likely author, and chose to confront the person at an organising meeting held one evening in the Shepherd Street building.

As well as the usual Black community organisers, a visiting Quaker, Charlotte Meachim, and several union members, including Bob Pringle, and a Communist Party member, Denis Freney, were among the non-Aboriginal people present at this meeting. Without having to say a word or voice my accusation, Gary Foley took the floor and issued an apology to me on behalf of himself and others who had helped pen their vicious words. He gave no reason for their actions, but I suspected that they had been all sitting around one night, smoking dope, and someone came up with what they all, in a drug-induced haze, thought was a terrific idea. In the cold reality of day, however, they had regretted their actions and were into damage control. I was reputed to have a true and sharp tongue and no one wanted a few lashes, but still I was hurt.

While in the process of preparing for the trip, an

invitation had arrived through Chicka Dixon for ten or so Blacks to go to China. Chicka asked me to join the party he was putting together, but because of my previous commitment, and even though I yearned to travel with a Black group instead of alone, I felt obliged to decline. It seemed to me that this invitation, which had also been extended to Gary and his cohorts, had more to do with their change of mind than with anything I was likely to say or do. Suddenly everyone felt wanted and was going somewhere. Perhaps they realised there was no place for envy and jealousy in the work we were trying to do.

I shared with no one that I was hurt, not angered, by their stupid actions. All the anger I carried was directed towards white institutions and individuals responsible for committing or condoning or choosing to remain ignorant about the atrocities that had been perpetrated on me and on other Blacks. I had no anger left to spare to lay on any of the people who I saw as the victims.

Because the flight to England was so long, I had requested three free days upon my arrival in which to orient myself and recover. I was quite appalled, therefore, when I reeled out of Customs, jet-lagged and weary, to find a press conference had been set up for me. This event, unfortunately, set the pace for my visit and I was rushed all over the country, giving talks to any group that had organised a venue and audience.

My primary hosts on arrival were a couple, Mr and Mrs Canteri. I shared their upstairs flat in a large house converted to apartments. I was taken aback to find that, although Australians, their bathroom had been turned into a storeroom, which I understood to be an English habit. I had limited my obsessive showering, cut down from six to two times a day. Nevertheless, I was distraught when I realised it would be nigh impossible to shower even once a day while I was there. Carl Canteri professed himself to be of communist persuasion and was critical of my need for privacy and personal hygiene.

The program that had been organised for me was extensive, and included television, radio and magazine interviews as well as speeches at public venues and tertiary institutions. I arrived in September and an Australian election was to be held in December, so a large part of my work was intended to politicise Australian expatriates and encourage them to vote for a change of government. Labor had been in the wilderness for twenty-three years.

It may have been a slow season for the media in England because news of my visit was quickly picked up and I was on everything, including the front cover of *The Observer*'s colour magazine. A BBC television program, 'Late Night Line Up', usually segmented like 'Sixty Minutes', devoted an entire hour to an interview with me.

As well, quite early on, Abjab organisers were contacted by Lord Vestey, who wished to invite me to lunch for an opportunity to talk. He had recently been in Australia and had been horrified by a demonstration against his company during which Blacks had sat in the street wearing signs saying: 'Vesteys suck Black blood'. Unfamiliar with getting around London I took a taxi to the restaurant instead of travelling by underground, and arrived an hour late. Lord Vestey, a quite young man, however, was still waiting and lunch turned out to be a strange experience.

The restaurant he had chosen was expensive, and he said I could have anything I wished. Sensing my concern at the cost, he confided, 'The price of meat in England is ridiculous.' As I understood from research of his family's extensive global investments, they controlled the price of beef throughout the world. I was, therefore, very interested to hear his comment. We talked about the Gurindji People's strike on his property at Wave Hill, in the Northern Territory. He explained that he had been trying to excise land to return to the traditional owners for some years but had been prevented from doing so by the incumbent government. We also discussed the widespread incidence of sexual abuse of Aboriginal girls as young as seven on stations he owned, which had been documented in the book *The Vestey Story*, researched and published by the Australian Meatworkers Union. He admitted that he had learned of these allegations and was mortified. But it was obvious to me that he didn't feel personally responsible, though he said he would sack any of his employees if he found them to be in any way involved in these practices. He also said he would instruct his Australian manager to make a contribution to the Aboriginal Medical Service to assist with its work. In due time, a small cheque did, in fact, arrive.

Everything on the tour was going quite smoothly, if being run ragged can be considered smooth, when I travelled to Blackpool to attend an important Labour Party conference at which I met many people I had heard about. On my return to London Carl met me at the station, a most unusual event as I normally had to find my way around this strange city completely alone. He said we were going home by taxi, but before we left the station he wished to speak with me.

The police, he told me, had called at the house. He understood they had a warrant for my arrest on charges

of assisting an escapee. He had given them an approx-
imate time that I would be home and asked them to
come back then.

My mind went into overdrive. I did not know what
Carl was talking about, but I knew I had done nothing
illegal. I was angry that he had told the police the likely
time of my return. I asked him to ring his wife and tell
her I hadn't arrived, and to say that the next train was
due in a few hours. He did so reluctantly.

We sat in silence while I turned my brain to the
problem in hand. Eventually I asked Carl to ring his
wife again and ask if the police had returned and
whether she had passed on the mis-information. They
had just left so we leapt in a cab and made a dash to
the house. I hoped to be safely installed by the time
they came again.

I told Carl he was to tell the police I wasn't home,
that I hadn't returned on the later train, and he was
now expecting me to arrive perhaps the next day. He
replied that neither he nor his wife were happy to tell
lies to protect me, not even to give me time to phone
Australia to find out what was going on.

Well, I thought, if Carl wasn't prepared to tell the
police I wasn't there, then the only thing I could do
was, in fact, *to not be there*. To their dismay I threw my
things into my suitcase and walked out of their house
into the night.

I had no money and didn't know a soul, apart from
the acquaintances I had made in the process of doing
media interviews. One of these, Peter Foges, the producer of 'Late Night Line Up', however, had been particularly kind and interested. From a phone box a few
blocks away from the flat I called the television station.
When he came on the line I was brief. His program was

due to go to air in a few minutes and he had little time to talk. He said finding alternative accommodation for me would be no problem, and proposed his mother's house or that of an ex-girlfriend. He explained that these would be open to me even if I was in trouble with the police. He asked me to take a cab to the house of some other friends of his, and he would come by as soon as he had finished work.

When I was ensconced in the house owned by his mother, I rang Carl's flat daily, without giving him a clue as to my whereabouts, to inquire if he had received any further information. I also rang home.

It was being alleged that on my way to England I had travelled via Perth, where I was supposed to have lodged a large sum of money into the account of Lionel Brockman for him to use to escape. Other rumours abounded. I was supposed to have hired a light plane and left it near the prison. I was supposed to have supplied him with cars and all manner of other things. A warrant for my arrest had been taken out by the Western Australian Government, though presumably the government would have given the papers to the Federal Police in Canberra in order for the London police to be acting on them. I was deeply alarmed.

News of the threat I was under obviously went out on the grapevine, because I was surprised to receive a message from a man in London I didn't know, a lawyer, Benedict Birnberg. Some years before, I learned, he had assisted in the defence of Richard Walsh, my old boss at *Nation Review*, and Richard Neville, during their trial for obscenity regarding their magazine, Oz. He had maintained his interest in Australia and was offering to defend me for free.

I went alone by cab to a darkened house in a

suburban area, the address Benedict Birnberg had given me on the phone. I was loath to let the cab go because there appeared to be no one at home. When I knocked, however, the door opened a crack and I slipped into the dim hall. Mr Birnberg ushered me into an office, where only a table lamp burned to relieve the gloom. We talked.

Mr Birnberg had a good sense of the dramatic and, having learned that I was scheduled to give a public address at the London Town Hall in a few days, he suggested that I remain in hiding until that date. If the police were going to arrest me, we should engineer for them to do it there in front of the expected large audience. He could, he promised, stave off an extradition order for a month or six weeks, and have me released on bail for a period. This would create the opportunity for me to use a very public platform from which I could talk about the persecution of my people, using my own arrest as an example. He would, he said, be present in the audience at the Town Hall, though not conspicuously. He would only emerge if his services were needed.

I was not the only speaker scheduled to make an address that night, but even so I was surprised at the huge audience of several hundreds which greeted me when I arrived. I was to share the platform with Mervyn Hartwig, Professor Fred Rose and Hannah Middleton. So many attended that they were unable to fit everyone into the auditorium and had to seat some in a nearby room where they could hear but not see, and to where we were asked to adjourn after the address to give the overflow a chance to talk with us.

I was extremely nervous and on edge as I made my way towards the stage, and every hand that reached out to either wave or welcome me I suspected was that of a plainclothes police officer.

Unbeknown to me, however, at home in Australia some journalists had gone to work and had investigated the basis of the charges being made against me. They found, of course, that these charges were completely without foundation, that I had not even been in Western Australia for almost a year, that no plane had been used in Lionel's walkout of the minimum security prison in which he had been housed, and any money that had been sent had been quite openly mailed to Lionel's wife to help her with the expenses of the children.

Whatever happened to the charges, warrant and extradition order, I have no idea. They were never served. I came off the platform at the London Town Hall and had coffee with friends before returning to the home of the television producer's mother. I then continued with my other public speaking commitments and no one ever approached me.

Mum and other members of my family at home in Australia had opened their newspapers one day to find my name on the front page. 'BOBBI SYKES SOUGHT IN ENGLAND', the headlines proclaimed. Mum almost had a heart attack. William felt himself justified in keeping Russel and Naomi away from me. I was a bad mother and not worthy of them. I struggled with the knowledge that I might have an enormous fight on my hands to convince any court that I was law-abiding and upstanding. I felt a great urge to see the little ones, to let them know I was not the bogey-man that these articles projected me to be.

I threw myself even harder into my work, agreeing to give talks in increasingly remote towns and villages around England. During these travels I was scheduled to arrive in Birmingham, go on to speak at Warwick, then return the next day to give an address at the Birmingham venue. I was unaware that there was anything extraordinary about this leg of the tour until I was already on the train. I had been surprised and indeed a little suspicious in London when I was told that an Abjab organiser would accompany me part of the way.

The young organiser disappeared to another carriage and I was left alone to read my book, but he returned as we reached our destination. He had something he wanted to tell me, he said, something he thought I should know. A Black group had put their hands up to be the local organisers of my presentation in Birmingham, but Abjab contacts had thought they might not have been able to attract a sufficiently large audience and had instead given the task to a white group.

Members of the Black group had gone to the office a couple of times to raise their objections, and on the last occasion had become enraged and assaulted people including, according to the organiser, a pregnant woman. I thought this was fine news to be presenting me with just as the train was pulling into the station. My estimation of Abjab's organisational ability was quickly revised downwards. I was, he said, to be on my guard. The upshot of all this was that there were now to be two presentations in Birmingham.

A car whisked us away to Warwick, where Germaine Greer had agreed to share the platform at my public talk. She had also invited me to stay at her house nearby in Coventry overnight before returning to Birmingham.

The meeting was held in a tiered auditorium with swing doors leading outside. We had not long started our presentation when these doors were swung open to reveal a group of Blacks, in the main, men. One was wearing a high crocheted cap in bright colours and when, with an exaggerated theatrical gesture, he took off this cap his long Rastafarian dreads whipped out. I didn't need two guesses to know who these people were.

Our talk was stopped by this sudden interruption and I was anxious to keep the peace and to get things back on track again, so I said, 'Welcome, Brothers. Please take a seat,' and gestured towards the auditorium. From behind me came a loudly hissed comment: 'Black male chauvinist pigs are as bad as white male chauvinist pigs.' Germaine! I could have happily strangled her. Fortunately if the Rastafarians had heard her remark they decided to ignore it.

When the presentation resumed the Rastafarians began to gently snipe, asking me inappropriate questions designed, I thought, to elicit whether or not I had known about Abjab's refusal to allow them to organise a meeting. I replied that we would have plenty of time to talk later, and would they please keep their questions until then.

At the conclusion of the presentations, organisers took up a collection to cover costs and make a contribution towards the Aboriginal program I had talked about. Although it was not really my business, I took charge of the cloth bag in which the notes and coins had been placed. Outside I could see the Rastafarians milling and I wanted, at all costs, to avoid more trouble, and I felt a gesture of my goodwill was necessary to ensure that end. I took the bag over to them, told them I was having dinner with a friend and asked them to mind the bag for me until the next day. Surprise swept over their faces immediately, and I could see that my action had stirred their respect. I also knew that not one penny would be missing. We all went off quietly on our respective ways.

Germaine had a young pregnant woman living with her, and she told me she was looking forward to playing a parenting role. 'I'll be Papa,' she laughed, and said she was taking driving lessons to prepare for the part. After a pleasant dinner, the young woman went off to her room and Germaine and I sat by the fire with our legs stretched out before us, talking of many things, including our arrests, which had transpired since we had first met. We were like two old soldiers discussing the glories of our battles and our war wounds.

Next day in Birmingham I gave a presentation to a rather small white audience; the room had more empty chairs than full ones. I was almost concluding when a couple of Rastafarians arrived—they had arranged for me to spend the afternoon at their organisation before giving the presentation they had organised for the evening. They laughed and one shook his finger at an organiser over the tiny size of the audience he had attracted, but otherwise they seemed in good humour.

The Rastas had arranged for me to speak in a community hall. It had plywood windows that could be propped open on sticks, which reminded me very much of buildings at home. We arrived early and when people, mainly West Indians and Africans, began to roll in I was very pleased with the extent of their interest. The hall was filled to capacity with adults and many children, and despite it being a very cold evening, a lot of others who were unable to fit in the hall stood outside peering in through the windows.

While the rest of the tour went off without any more

upsets, I became increasingly distraught about the possibility of returning to Australia under the existing government, which had already demonstrated its hostile intent towards me. I hoped that the widespread efforts to bring about a change of government would be effective. However, I also began making discreet inquiries, in case they should fail, in the hope of a country offering me asylum. I feared I may have had to wait out a further term of the incumbents' tenure before another attempt to dislodge them could be made. Because of all the things I had already witnessed and heard, I frankly feared for my life and certainly for my freedom if I was to return to Australia.

I started to make the rounds of a few African embassies, some of whose citizens had attended my presentations and had indicated to me that they thought their governments were sympathetic with the Black Australian cause.

Talk of the threat of my arrest had travelled widely, I found, and representatives at some embassies bluntly told me to go away. Even my presence at their offices was being construed as some sort of threat; it might draw the attention of police, might upset their aid relationship with Australia. I was disheartened. Tanzania, I'd been told, had a reputation for extending shelter to people, but that office also turned me down. Nigeria, which was one of the countries I hadn't approached, contacted me and told me that I would be welcome there.

Around this time, while travelling to one of my rural engagements, I read in an English newspaper that the Aboriginal China tour was underway, and the report said the group was presently in Red Square. The thought of Cheryl Buchanan, Chicka and Gary discussing everything they saw and laughing together at the end of the day was in sharp contrast to my own isolation, and I burst into tears. Other passengers stared at me coldly.

The idea that I may have to abandon my life in Australia completely continued to cause me great stress. I was, by then, staying with Lynne and John Roberts, who were associated with Abjab. Lynne was well-known, had her own business and lived in a wealthy area of London, and I felt very safe under her aegis. I thought the police would be less likely to make another move against me while I was at her house. Everyone in her family was helpful and supportive towards me, and Lynne, noticing that I felt the bitter cold through the short cotton coat that Bruce McGuinness had taken off his back and given me for the trip, took me to a store and fitted me out in a wool-lined suede coat with pants to match. This generous gesture helped me overcome some of the very negative feelings I had about being in England.

Abjab decided it would be appropriate for me to travel to the US where I could try to interest representatives at the United Nations in our plight. I had already made one side trip, to Switzerland, where I met, amongst others, the Reverend Charles Spivey at the World Council of Churches. He had introduced me to Andrew Young, who would much later become the first Black US Ambassador to the United Nations.

In New York I first stayed at the flat of a young white Australian, Mark Lazaros, an ophthalmology student, who was somehow known to Abjab members. At the Methodist Mission to the United Nations I met an outgoing Black woman, Melba Smith, who invited me to stay at her place in Harlem. Under her guidance I was able to establish contact with a range of United Nations people, many of whom, unfortunately, turned out to be more interested in chatting me up than in taking a political interest in the conditions of Blacks in Australia.

I was in New York in December 1972 when the federal elections were held in Australia. I rang the Australian Consul's office many times to try to get the results. Failing this, I then phoned some Australian media offices and, almost despairing at the disinterest exhibited by these expatriate reporters, finally learned that Labor, under Gough Whitlam's leadership, had won. I felt enormously relieved. I could at last go home.

On my return to London, en route to Australia, my hosts, Lynne and John Roberts, organised a farewell party for me on my last night. At the height of the celebrations, at which there were many people who were strangers to me, I was approached by a man who, it turned out, was an Australian journalist. 'Don't you remember me?' he asked. 'I'm from Townsville. I used to stone you when you were little.'

I went into shock. Emotions and scenes from these childhood stonings flashed through my mind, mixed with emotions and memories of having been raped, beaten and left to die in the bush. My stomach turned over and, despite the bitterly cold London winter's night, I walked out of my own party and prowled the streets for hours. When I came back and found the house in darkness, I slipped in to wash, rest and pack. I was on my way home.

9

My plane arrived in Sydney on the final day of a ten-day heatwave. I welcomed the simmering weather after my long sojourn out in the cold. Things in my flat looked askew. I soon found that my little address book full of international contacts was missing from a tiny space under the bottom drawer of the desk where I had concealed it. I would later discover passages of letters from Lionel Brockman to me had been printed in some newspapers. I asked the woman who lived next door if she had seen anyone entering my flat, and she had. She had watched two plain clothes men, she thought were police, go into my place.

I had written from London to Eric Strasser asking him to begin action so I could gain access to my children, and just over a week later William flew them down. I was so happy to see them and they to see me. I had brought them back clothes, toys and kites. We walked to nearby Moore Park to fly their kites on days when there was sufficient breeze. Eric and his wife Dee spent a day helping me entertain them, and Russel raved over Eric's car, a Jaguar.

William rang every day the children were with me, not to speak to them but to be reassured that I intended to send them back. Over the time, however, I noticed a slight change in his conversation, a move from 'send them back' to 'bring them back'. When I picked up on it, I said he had sent them in the care of a flight attendant, and I would do this too. No, he responded, I was to bring them. He would pay for my round trip ticket. To avoid further hassles I agreed, on the proviso that he arrange for me to stay elsewhere overnight other than at Mum's house where he still lived.

I felt William regarded this as some sort of test. Would I, after spending a few weeks with my children, be able to leave them again? This stiffened my resolve to get custody of the children and stay in Sydney. After accompanying them home, talking with William and staying overnight with his friends, I hugged and kissed both children warmly.

Very shortly after this, William phoned again. He said he was putting Russel and Naomi on the next plane. Having to care for the children would stop me running around the world making trouble. Russel had mentioned to him about 'the man with the Jaguar' and, quick to assume that Eric was more than my solicitor and friend, William was very displeased. I had always believed it was inevitable that William would pass the children over to me and, not wishing to involve them in a legal tug of war, I'd just bided my time.

My bedsitter was too small for anything more than

a visit from the children, I told him. I'd need two weeks in which to find a more suitable place.

While certainly true, there were other reasons why I did not want William to send the children down immediately. My phone number and address had been listed in the phone book under my name and I had, over the period of my occupancy, received a number of racist crank calls, including several death threats. A molotov cocktail had been left at my door, and other unsuccessful efforts made to kill or frighten me. During the children's visit I had reasoned that, having just spent three months in England, the chance anyone knew yet that I was home was remote. After being back in Australia for a while though, the danger would return and increase. I would have to pay greater attention to the children's security than I ever had to my own.

As well, the day after William rang me I was leaving to attend a regional planning committee meeting being held in Jamaica for the Sixth Pan-African Congress. I had received a call a few days earlier from a man, Roderick Francis, who had just returned to Jamaica from London. While in the UK he had read reports on my tour and, through one of the organisers, had located my number in Australia. In Jamaica, he had urged the conference to include the South Pacific region as part of the 'Black world', suggesting that I might be a likely representative.

Roderick turned out to be a wealthy eccentric who lived in a large rambling dirt-floor shack on a dairy farm which he owned. The New Zealand Dairy Company, he told me, had bought out the only milk processing plant on the island and closed it down, forcing farmers to sell their dairy cows to American farmers.

New Zealand then began to export its dairy products to Jamaica. Roderick had held out against this.

Aged about eighty, he had seen an electric organ in England and decided he wanted to learn to play it. He had installed a wooden floor in one room to give the instrument stability, and he had electricity connected to just that one room. When he heard that I played keys, we spent a happy half hour or more playing duets, much to the amusement of the other delegates he was hosting.

I met many very significant people at this meeting, including Carlos Moore, who had been a Minister in Castro's Cabinet but was living in exile in France at the time; Abdias di Nascimento, then in exile in the US but later to resume his position as the only Black senator in Brazil; and Mrs Garvey, widow of Marcus Garvey, leader of a broadbased 'Back to Africa' movement throughout the West Indies and North America. Mrs Garvey later organised for the speech I presented there to be published in an American magazine, *Black World*. It was the first article I had ever had published outside Australia.

The Australian Test Cricket team was in Jamaica when I arrived, and on the second evening Rastafarians came to the conference to inform me of the cricketers' outrageous behaviour and sexual indiscretions. Wherever they played, I was told, they left a crop of 'cricket babies' to be born to young teenage girls who were unable to look after them. The strain on their families, I heard, was enormous, and the girls were scorned, their life chances diminished. As the majority of people of colour in Jamaica were poor, I was upset and ashamed to learn that white Australians were contributing to their poverty by refusing to acknowledge and support the women they impregnated and the babies they created. Other West Indians present agreed that this practice was not limited to Jamaica.

We talked, too, about the position of Blacks in Australia, and the Rastas asked me to write out some information on these conditions. A speedy writer, I quickly jotted down five or six pages of notes as I had all the information, including statistics, in my head.

The next night high-ranking police came to my hotel to question me. Did I know, they asked, that Rastas had that day handed out information sheets about conditions faced by Australian Aborigines outside the cricket ground? Did I, in fact, write the flier?

They warned me that if I wrote any more sheets I would be in serious trouble. The flier they showed me contained only a fraction of the information I had already written up, and I agreed not to write any more.

They came back the following night to show me another information sheet, and inquire if I was the author. This time they told me I was placing their country in a difficult position, because Jamaica and Australia were both members of the Commonwealth. Their prime minister did not want to do anything to embarrass Australia, which these revelations on Aboriginal conditions would surely do.

On my last night in the country, senior police came again with yet another handout and told me they had no option but to deport me. I wasn't afraid, although I could see they were grim. I informed them then of the political situation in Australia, how our government had recently changed through an election which Prime Minister Manley may not yet have heard about. I said that the present government would not be embarrassed by health, education, unemployment and environmental conditions described in the fliers. It would condemn them as the work of the previous government, which had been in power for the last twenty-three years. My deportation, I added, would be an embarrassment, for Jamaica not for Australia. If they were determined to deport me, I continued, even though I had planned to leave the next day, I'd be happy to wait a few more days to give them time to process their paperwork.

The police apologised and I left the next day. Following comments I made after my return I was contacted by a courageous person, Graeme Orr, who had previously played international cricket for Australia. He had left the game, he said, because he'd been unable to tolerate the racist behaviour of his fellow players.

On arriving back from Jamaica, I changed planes in Sydney and flew to Canberra where a Black conference had been convened. Arriving on its second day, I was concerned to hear that 'Islanders' had been expelled from the meeting. 'Who's doing this, and how are they deciding who is an Islander?' I asked the first person I met there. 'Sydney Blacks are behind this, and it's on hair,' I was told.

I was hit with the sharp memory of this same modus of separation which had occurred at St Joseph's Orphanage in Rockhampton when I was a child. Brother and sister, separated; members of the same family, separated—on the basis of their straight or curly hair. It was hard to believe Blacks were now doing the same thing to each other. I walked into the auditorium where the conference was being held and sat down.

On the platform I saw many of the familiar faces,

and in the first few rows sat a number of traditional Aboriginal people, mainly men. I listened to the proceedings, which seemed quite ordinary. The expulsions of the previous day were not mentioned. Kevin Gilbert, no longer on parole and consequently able to travel to Canberra, came up to sit beside me, and I whispered to him what I had heard.

'Those fellows,' he said, indicating the people who sat on the stage, 'made the tribal people think that after they fought to get their land off the white fellahs, they'd have to fight to get it off the Islanders too. Not everyone here agrees—but no one wants to be seen to oppose the traditional people. You know how it is.'

'So what about me?'

'You're with me,' Kevin responded. 'You've been one of us since the beginning, and if they put you out they put me out too.' Although I appreciated Kevin's gesture of friendship, I asked him politely to move away. He knew the reason—I wanted to see if anyone was going to say anything about my hair and, if so, I didn't want his presence to deter them.

During the morning tea break I saw Faith Bandler, who I'd learned was one of the people expelled from the conference, talking earnestly in the foyer. She was with her old FCAATSI colleague, Gordon Bryant, the new Minister for Aboriginal Affairs in the Labor government. Faith, I thought, had been in the struggle before many of these young Turks were even born. We had reached a very sad day in Black affairs!

After this episode I began to seriously question some of the dicta of the Black movement. The cry for 'Black unity and solidarity', it seemed to me, was being manipulated. It was trotted out in the main to prevent Blacks who were being victimised within the movement from discussing their pain with outsiders. Sayings such as, 'Don't argue in front of whites' and 'Keep Black things in-house' were being evoked in an effort to create an unjust class structure even within the group active in the struggle against inequality.

I determined then to work with those Kooris who I felt were doing honest and important work, not armchair critics. I would leave alone those people driven by goals of complete self-interest who promoted separatism. Unity and solidarity were important, but it was equally important to sort out how these ideas were to be used effectively. Otherwise they threatened to become vehicles for severe social disruption within the Black community. Dispossession and the *concept* of justice through land rights, for example, were critical issues that needed to be supported and promoted by everyone, black and white. However, advocacy of these issues did not mean that all supporters and promoters, themselves, intended to make land claims.

Discrimination, selective prosecution and imprisonment, racism and racist violence were amongst the issues that affected every black person, and there was a great need in these areas for unity and solidarity to break these things down. Although I stayed on for the duration of the conference, I left very disheartened.

On my return to Sydney I received yet another blow. Ian rang from Melbourne to inform me that, in my absence, he had attended a party where he had heard me being defamed. The Minister for Science and External Territories, Mr William Morrison, had told a roomful of people that I would go far, that I'd slept my way to the top. Ian had been astounded and challenged the minister. In response, Mr Morrison had listed names of politicians or their family members with whom he claimed I had had affairs. Ian made a note of the names, and spoke to other people at the party who were prepared to go to court on my behalf if I wanted to sue. Furthermore, he had made a cursory check of the list to find that a politician's son, with whom the minister had alleged I had had intimate relations, was only twelve years old. Mr Morrison had concluded his attack by saying to Ian, 'What's the matter with you? Aren't you getting yours?' Ian was livid and urged me to take action.

I considered all the people who had worked so hard to help bring about a change of government, and all the people who I hoped would benefit. The new government had been in power just two months. Would I be the first to try to bring it down, after all that I had gone through to help it gain power? Yet I had to do something. I didn't know Mr Morrison, and couldn't fathom why he would make such false accusations against me, not to mention sullying the names of his Labor Party colleagues.

I wrote him a letter.

Dear Mr Morrison, I am aware that at XYZ address and at this specific time, in the company of Messrs A, B and C, and witnessed by D, E and F, you did make the following remarks about me.

As well as advising him that I was sending copies of my letter to all the people whose name he had mentioned, I demanded an apology. I further told him that his behaviour was sexist and racist, and that as the position of Minister for External Territories would bring him into contact with non-white countries, especially Papua New Guinea, I regarded him as totally unfit for the job.

In addition to the men whose names he had

mentioned, I sent a copy of my letter to Gough Whitlam's wife, Margaret. While I chose not to make a formal complaint, I wanted the matter dealt with broadly in-house, not swept under the carpet.

The only response I received was from Barry Cohen, MP, who had been a familiar figure around the Aboriginal Embassy and was known by almost everyone there. He phoned to tell me Mr Morrison had been confronted by many of his parliamentary colleagues, that the only excuse he had offered was that he was drunk at the time, and that he was now living in fear of reading a newspaper in case he should find the matter on the front page.

Although I knew of a great many people and women's organisations, such as WEL, which would have been very interested to know of this incident, I did not inform them. Someone, though, did leak the information, and a small report about my letter appeared in the limited-circulation newspaper *Private Eye*.

I had just three days left to find accommodation in which I could welcome my children. In *Nation Review* I found an advertisement placed by a family in Gladesville who wished to share their house. I rang them and, being *Nation Review* readers, they immediately recognised my name.

The house was large, and the two bedrooms on offer were not very close together. Still, Russel was twelve and Naomi five, so they were old enough to come looking for me in the night if need arose. I met the children at the airport and we moved in. Although I was a bit sorry to give up the convenient location of my flat, I was so overjoyed with having my children with me at last that no sacrifice was too great.

At this time I imposed on the AMS to create a position for me. I had been working on a voluntary basis for the organisation for over a year and had raised substantial funds for the service. Now, Federal Government funding was assured, but there remained the need to generate both publicity and private funds to enable the service to retain a degree of autonomy and not come under complete government control. I became education/publicity officer and, using my extensive list of contacts, wrote and circulated a regular newsletter. I also successfully approached vitamin and blanket manufacturers to contribute goods to help needy Kooris make it through the bleak winter. The Ford Motor Company heard of my work and contacted me. For months they kept me supplied with a vehicle, and Ampol donated petrol to keep it on the road. This enabled me to respond to urgent requests from communities as far south as Lake Tyers in Victoria, as well as several areas in New South Wales.

The service had a long and expensive wrangle with South Sydney Council, which claimed that the presence of the AMS in Redfern *attracted* Blacks to the area (rather than providing a service for the thousands who already lived here). As a consequence, the AMS moved from its original two-room shopfront to a slightly larger premises a few doors down, still on Regent Street. Despite greater privacy and better medical facilities for patients, the administration section was particularly cramped and there was no office or even a desk for me.

I received a call from Dr Moss Cass, the Federal Minister for the Environment, requesting a meeting.

He came early one morning to the AMS, and because I didn't have an office I invited him into Naomi Mayers' office to talk. He was hardly seated when Naomi arrived. I hastened to introduce her.

'What are you doing in here?' she boomed.

'Naomi, I'd like you to meet Dr Moss Cass.'

'I don't care who he is. Get him out of here. I want to work.'

I found it difficult to believe Naomi hadn't noticed his government limousine and driver parked directly outside the building. I had to apologise to him and try to make light of the incident, then Dr Cass and I adjourned to a nearby milkbar and had a cup of tea. He invited me to join an environment advisory committee he was putting together, the membership of which had not yet been finalised but which would include the unionist, Mr John Halfpenny, representatives from CSIRO and other scientific, development and regulatory bodies. As I was both interested and widely read in the area of environmental science, I agreed.

On my return to the AMS I told Naomi exactly who she had just booted out of her office.

'A politician? We're not about politics,' she replied. 'This service is about health.'

Despite the frustration I often felt at the low level of political nous and the lack of support I received, I continued working at the AMS, generating literature, sponsorship and funds, as well as responding to many rural communities' requests for information when they wanted to start their own medical services. I also took my place on the Environmental Advisory Committee, and despite the intensive reading this often required, I enjoyed the intellectual stimulation of a diverse committee concentrating on one point of common concern—the environment. My work day was long and in the evenings I often had to bring the children in with me to Redfern to attend meetings. They frequently went to sleep on the floor.

Around this time I received a letter from the Taxation Department, forwarded to me by William. It was a final notice, informing me of the department's intention to arrest and imprison me for non-payment after seven days. The week's notice had already been exceeded by more than three days by the time it arrived. William, I learned, had signed my name on documents to turn my half of the company over to him and the department was wanting their share of my profits. I panicked and rang Eric. He contacted the department on my behalf and obtained an extension. I was fortunate then to meet an accountant, Rob Fisher, who helped explain to the department that I had never received any money from the company and indeed had even lost my initial investment.

I rang William. He admitted not having forwarded the Tax Department's earlier correspondence, and seemed unconcerned that his actions had brought me to the brink of imprisonment, which would have left the children without care. I thought my explanation to the department may have put him in trouble, and was surprised at his disinterest. 'I'm going bankrupt anyway,' he told me, which I found difficult to believe as he had just recently bought a speedboat.

At home I began to notice strange things. The couple who shared the house were both psychiatric nurses and worked shifts, and another woman often seemed to be there. At our weekly house meeting I was informed that the woman had moved in. She was sharing the master bedroom with the couple, and they were 'exploring an alternative lifestyle'.

I wrote to Mum and she and Arthur came down, bringing their caravan and parking it in the backyard. Despite having a job which enabled me to pay the rent and fit the children out with schoolwear, I had made little progress establishing a secure domestic base. The other family must have taken their family's clothes to launder at the hospitals where they worked, as there was no washing machine in the house, and I was obliged to do all our washing by hand, a long and tiresome job. Mum took over the washing for me one day to give me time to run out and look for a second-hand washing machine. When I returned she advised me that the family I was sharing with was too strange, and that I should move.

Leonie had rented a flat in Ernest Street, Crows Nest, but was planning to give it up. 'Take over her place,' Mum urged me, 'and do it while we're here so we can give you a hand to shift your things.' Ford's contribution of a vehicle had by then petered out and I didn't own a car.

After two weeks in the Crows Nest flat, I presented myself at the real estate agent and told him I was Leonie's sister and wanted to take over her lease. Because of Leonie's Asian features and very straight silky hair, I was initially met with open disbelief over my statement that we were related, but eventually the agent said, 'I heard you were there. You've kept the place clean and you've paid the rent. You can stay.'

I heard later that the man in the domestic triangle at the Gladesville house had committed suicide. He had shot himself in the head. I thought of the two women and small children he had left behind. What would become of them now?

I enrolled Russel at Crows Nest Boys' High and Naomi at Cammeray Primary. My wages from AMS barely covered our expenses, so I had to continue to write articles and review books to supplement our income.

William came down to Sydney at this time, and when he saw how we were living he offered to buy me a car. I was outraged at the idea that he could cheat me out of my half of the business and then offer to patronise me, placing me in the position of having to accept a 'gift'.

'Just give me the money you owe me and I'll be able to buy my own car,' I responded.

'Okay. If that's how you feel about it, you'll get nothing,' he said as he departed.

In adversity, I threw myself into even more work. Taking the children with me at night to AMS management meetings meant having to wake Russel and make him walk while carrying Naomi in my arms. We would catch a train to Wynyard, where we changed to a bus that would take us almost to our door. I also sat up nights, reviewing books and writing articles, surviving for weeks on four hours sleep a night.

I received a brief letter from Charles, the Black American soldier who had befriended me when I'd first arrived in Sydney. He alerted me to an article in either *Penthouse* or *Playboy* in which, he said, 'your friend has betrayed you'. Unable to afford such expensive magazines, I went to several newsagencies to read the article.

Germaine had written a piece on rape. In it, as I

recall, she inferred that women who had been raped and who didn't make it public were doing a disservice to the women's movement. She referred to a few examples including my own, using the scant details I had shared with her. Although she did not disclose my name, the description she gave was sufficient for my friend to identify me. In conclusion the article said that she intended to give the names of the women next time.

I was stunned. How could I have been so naive and trusting? I fumed. And how could Germaine so easily betray my confidence, throw into the public arena information I had shared with her so privately?

I staggered home under the heavy weight of her disloyalty, weeping at my own stupidity. I was to blame, I reasoned. If I had answered with a lie when she had asked me so directly, this would not have occurred.

Heavily into forgiveness at the time, I tried to excuse Germaine, telling myself that she could have no idea of how much harm her disclosure could do to an innocent child, Russel. Despite my efforts to put the article behind me—it was published in the US, few people would read it in Australia, and there was little likelihood anyone else would have made the connection—I remained angry. How could anyone, much less a feminist, treat personal confidences with such disdain as to put them into print for mere money? After this incident, every time I was approached by white women reputed to be feminists, suspicion and distrust arose in my mind and, in many instances, I closed off any possibility of friendship with them. I could not afford to be hurt again. I could not afford relationships that might ill-effect my son.

Just as I was beginning to find juggling all my

commitments an almost impossible task, an amazing stroke of good fortune occurred. While giving a talk to a North Shore women's group, I was approached by one of the participants, Mrs Mary Owen, who said she lived close by me and would be interested to help if she could.

A few days later, MumShirl called and asked me to attend to a young woman who was suicidal. I rang Mrs Owen to ask if she would mind looking after Russel and Naomi for a few hours, as I had to deal with an emergency. Mrs Owen, whose own children were grown up, was reluctant; she had not expected that I would ask her for assistance with childcare. Her husband, she told me, didn't like children—but, 'well, since it's an emergency'.

Neither Mrs Owen nor I were prepared for Mr Owen's complete reversal. A taciturn man with few friends, he was perhaps won over by Russel's thoughtful consideration of everything that was said to him and Naomi's happiness just to bubble along chatting even if she received no reply. It was not long before Mr Owen himself was knocking on my door, asking if my children could go to the beach or a local fete with him. Russel and Naomi became regular guests at their house, welcome at any time of the day or night. I encouraged the children to consider the Owens as extended family members, putting them on our gift list for Mother's Day and Christmas. Over time Mr and Mrs Owen became as close as grandparents.

With Mrs Owen's assistance I was able do even more work for the AMS and take on many of the tasks MumShirl was anxious to pass over to me.

I wrote a report on the philosophy and activities of the AMS for a review in Canberra, and was unhappy to find my name taken off it to be replaced with Naomi Mayers' and Paul Coe's names. Naomi told me Paul would have objected to taking a report to the government under my name, but I suspected he had not even been asked. As neither Naomi nor Paul had laid eyes on the work until it was completely finished, I considered the action as intellectual appropriation and said so. When the work became widely quoted in many other documents within government circles, with Naomi and Paul cited as the authors, I began to wonder if either of them felt any embarrassment.

Government subsidisation enabled the AMS to increase the salaries of Black workers to bring them into line with their white equivalents. As the only Black worker whose salary was not increased, I prevailed upon Naomi, as administrator, to put a case on my behalf to the Board for their consideration. When she refused to do so, I resigned.

With my only regular income gone, I raced around trying to find more work, without any great success. Although I had formally resigned from the AMS, I was still called upon when my skills or contacts were required.

The government had promised the AMS a permanent home, as the building it occupied was under threat of demolition. When a suitable building was finally located, no easy feat in the limited area of their search, AMS Board representatives went to Canberra to discuss its purchase. However, they were told the building was too expensive. As no financial parameters had previously been mentioned, when they queried the ceiling they were informed the building was just $20,000 over the mark. Sister Ignatius rang me on behalf of the AMS, asking me what I thought I could do.

I contacted one of Ian's friends in Melbourne, Sandra Bardas, who had already shown deep interest and support in a wide range of Black community endeavours. Her husband, David, owned Sportsgirl, a chain of clothing stores around Australia.

Within forty-eight hours I had in my hand an offer from Sportsgirl to make up the difference, if the government would proceed with the purchase. The offer stipulated that the AMS should be the outright owners, and that Sportsgirl retained the right to publicise their contribution.

On receipt of this offer, the government turned around and agreed to fund the entire purchase. Although the government then stalled the acquisition so long that this particular deal fell through, the AMS had been able to demonstrate its ability to bring its own strengths to the negotiating table.

The work of the AMS, I had decided, was too important for personality differences and petty jealousies to prevent the essential teamwork required for its success. I continued to oblige whenever I was called upon, displaying, I hoped, a loyalty that would eventually gain acknowledgement if not reward.

We were unable to live on the little money I was now earning so, without any great hope, I rang William to see if he was prepared to pay maintenance. He was blunt. The answer was no.

'I have no responsibility for Russel anyway,' he informed me.

I reminded him that he had adopted the boy and that this had established a legal responsibility for his welfare.

'If you're going to come at that, I'll tell him how he

really came to be here,' he replied. Threatened with disclosure of the one thing he knew I did not want Russel to know, at least until he was old enough to understand, I backed off. I felt this was about as low as a man could go in order to get out of providing food for his children.

With no other options left to me, I realised I would have to go to the government and plead my case for a supporting mother's benefit. Recalling my distress when, years earlier, I had required assistance, I agonised over this decision and determined that I would tell the Social Security staff only as much as they needed to know.

In the department's office, on the day of my appointment, I had a sense of tension in the air, but couldn't work out why. My interview was conducted by a woman, Suzy Hayes, who was warm and helpful.

I was surprised when, a very short time later, Suzy rang asking if I would meet her for a drink after work.

We met in a small coffee lounge in Wynyard where Suzy told me frankly that she was the 'trouble-shooter' for the department, called upon to conduct interviews at which it was anticipated that there might be trouble or disruption. Parents accompanied by their difficult intellectually disabled adolescent children and people who could not control their charges were typical of the clients she was allocated for interview. She was aghast that she had been sent to interview me. Suzy had not known who I was when she received my file, and her supervisors had advised her to leave the door of the interview room open, and back-up had been stationed in the hallway. No wonder I had felt some tension.

I couldn't help laughing, even though I felt outraged beneath my mirth. None of these people knew me, I thought. What sort of image is the media projecting of me?

Suzy became a good friend and, over time, we shared meals and I listened to her talk about her dissatisfaction with the way the department functioned. One day she came to me with a copy of a notice from the bulletin board which announced a review of departmental procedures and invited submissions. She would like, she told me, to put in a report but didn't have the ability to write anything so comprehensive.

'You have all the info,' I suggested to her, 'and I can write. We could put our knowledge and skills together.'

Several late nights later, Suzy's damning report was prepared. In it, she exposed practices which included officers labelling trays containing applications for unmarried mothers' benefits with a tag saying 'Sluts', delaying processing applications for financial aid to people from specific ethnic groups, and generally hindering, confusing, or refusing by procrastination, services that should have been readily available to all Australian citizens in need.

Once word of her report became known, Suzy was demoted and sent to work on simple and repetitive clerical tasks in the basement of the building. Committee members of the Canberra review, however, invited her to meet with them in the capital. She was permitted out of the basement only long enough to attend this review hearing.

Major departmental policy changes flowed from Suzy's report. She was eventually transferred to a newly opened office in Redfern. Despite the vast improvement in the quality of service which her presence in this high need area created, Suzy suffered from restrictions which were imposed on her and ultimately she resigned.

It was around this time that Kevin Gilbert was arrested on charges of 'threatening to kill the Queen'. In the leadup to Queen Elizabeth II's visit to open the Sydney Opera House, staff at the *Australian* newspaper received a letter threatening her life. Kevin was subsequently arrested and charged. As he had previously served a life sentence for the murder of his first wife, a white woman, he was in a very disadvantaged position even though he was no longer even on parole.

About a month earlier, with great fanfare, some writer had released a novel about a group, Black October, in which fictional characters did make an assassination attempt during the opening of the Opera House. In the days immediately prior to the opening, many Black community organisers were arrested and detained in police lockups for the duration of the Queen's visit. We were concerned that police imagined some connection between this novel and real life, but there was little we could do about it.

After the Queen's departure, Kevin was released on a high bail which he was obliged to borrow from his father-in-law, a fact about which he spoke bitterly. I contacted Dominic Nagle, who was still working at the *Australian*. Dominic told me that the letter containing the threat had been opened, as were all letters to 'The Editor', by a mailboy who sorted the mail by quickly scanning the first few lines then placing them in piles depending on the category. When he'd seen 'Opera House', he had assumed the letter to be about music and the arts, and placed it in that pile.

After the letter's contents had been read by the receiving editor and found to contain a threat, the mailboy had been dispatched to find the envelope in which the letter had arrived. From a heap of discarded envelopes he had pulled one post-marked 'Newcastle'. Kevin lived in Taree. Apparently that was close enough. Throughout, Kevin maintained his innocence, and there was no physical evidence to link the letter with him. Despite this, he was placed in a position of anxiety and distress for months as he waited for the case to come to trial. Ultimately, however, the charge was abandoned, but not without having taken a grave toll on his health.

As Blacks, we lived with these abuses of power constantly and they caused us all a great deal of stress. I was invited to attend a conference at the World Council of Churches in Switzerland, after which I had arranged to go to another meeting in Nigeria, at the invitation of the planning committee for the Black World Arts and Culture Festival. For three days and nights prior to my departure, a marked police car was stationed directly outside my flat. The police officers made no attempt to molest me as I went about my business, but I was followed everywhere. I interpreted their presence to mean that they wanted me to know I was being watched. But why? When I left to catch my flight, my neighbours later informed me, the police car also left and was not seen again. What did it all mean?

With the pension Suzy had facilitated for me, I had gained a short breather from my financial anxiety. As well as continuing my involvement in educating the public on Black issues, and assisting Black individuals and organisations, I used the break to undertake a video operation course. It was offered to Black students through the then Australian Film and Television School, and was taught by Stuart Littlemore. I also took a short course in multi-camera van operation, but even at the time I realised how unlikely it would ever be for a Black to be entrusted with such expensive equipment.

In November, with Mrs Owen looking after the children, I was free to keep an appointment I had set up with people on Palm Island. At a conference earlier that year in Canberra, I had been approached by Iris Clay, wife of the Chair of the newly created Palm Island Aboriginal Council, which was meant to take over custodianship of the reserve, a former Aboriginal prison settlement. A mainland-based administrator had refused me permission to visit the island when I lived in Townsville. He had rolled a thick truncheon backwards and forwards across his desk while he told me, 'Blacks on Palm Island can't have visitors who are not under the Act. They might pick up the idea that they too could come and go as they please.'

Iris explained that big changes were occurring on the island, and that she and her husband, Fred, who was responsible for issuing permits, would welcome me. When I suggested my application for a permit to visit would never get to him as all correspondence was passed through the administration, Iris insisted we set a date immediately and that she and Fred would meet me at the air strip with my permit from the Council in their hands.

Iris was as good as her word. A policeman stationed on the island, who met every plane to check the passengers, snatched the permit as soon as Fred extended it to me, so I never actually got to read it. After a quick trip around to show me the layout of the reserve, we went to their house, one of only a few houses occupied by Blacks in the otherwise 'white' area of the settlement.

A line of Black residents immediately began to make their way to the house to meet me and tell me of their complaints. One family brought their son who had been thrashed by a teacher and had savage welt marks down his back and thighs. I suggested Fred take him to the doctor and get a certificate attesting to his injuries so that a formal complaint could be lodged. Fred brought back a simple statement stating the nature of the abrasions but omitting to mention they were consistent with the information given to him by the boy. When I told Fred I felt the doctor's two-line statement might be insufficient to be used as evidence, I realised that Fred's literacy skills as well as his procedural knowledge were very limited. Fred and Iris both pleaded with me to consider staying with them for a few months to help.

That night residents staged an impromptu concert to welcome me. Musicians brought their instruments along and set them up on the front porch. For a couple of hours, men, women and children sang and entertained us. Iris was so happy she had some lads shin up a coconut tree and attach a land-rights flag she had hand-sewn, modelled on the flag she had seen at the Embassy in Canberra. Two white female teachers sat on the grass amongst the assembled people throughout the evening, enjoying the good time which was being had by all.

Unbeknown to us, however, other white residents had called for a contingent of police to be flown in from the mainland, and armed vigilantes were summoned from a nearby rig. The whites barricaded themselves in the hospital, after discharging the Aboriginal patients, and armed themselves with all the weapons they could find on the island. Syringes were filled with ether to make flame-throwers. Police stationed marksmen in the surrounding hills, their weapons trained on us during the concert.

We were all fearful about these almost unbelievable developments. I felt a high degree of responsibility and slipped out of the house, making my way to the centre of the town where the only phone available to Blacks was located. I rang Senator Jim Keeffe's home in Townsville. Senator Keeffe was a well-known and active supporter of the struggle and the Embassy, and I knew him and his wife, Sheila, very well. I told Sheila what was going on and asked her to contact the press in the south. They were to ring me back on that public phone at ten the next morning.

When I returned to wait for these calls, a clerk informed me that the phone was 'out of order'. For three days we lived in fear, isolated from the outside world, watching the police and other white strangers who were watching us. Some white women were given firearms lessons in the town centre. I carried out investigations into conditions and took photos. On the fourth day I walked into an administration office and asked a clerk how long the phone would be out of order as I wished to ring the charter plane so I could leave. He promised to let me know as soon as it became operable. I had hardly taken two dozen steps down the dusty road when he came running up behind me.

'Excuse me, excuse me,' he called. 'The phone's fixed now. You can use it.'

I could barely believe how blatantly oppressive the place was, turning the phone off for the entire Black population in order to prevent me contacting journalists and federal politicians. That it was turned on again the moment I signalled my intention to leave confirmed how overtly they were prepared to operate, with complete impunity.

On the mainland I stayed in Margaret and Henry Reynolds' granny flat in their back garden for a few days. When I returned to the empty house from shopping one afternoon, I discovered all my film had been exposed, including the roll in the camera, which had been removed. ASIO or the police, I thought, were up to their old tricks again.

The *Townsville Daily Bulletin* carried a series of distorted reports of events on Palm Island, describing it as 'a riot' and presenting me in an extremely denigratory manner. The articles alleged, too, that I had brought the land-rights flag, described therein as a 'black power flag', up from Canberra. I spoke to Iris on the phone, and she wept. 'They won't even give me credit for being able to make a flag myself,' she sobbed.

I had learned a great deal about Palm Island during my visit. Asked to help residents with nutritional advice, I discovered there were no fresh vegetables (other than onions) or fruit in the government-run store. White residents, who numbered several hundred, had their groceries shipped over from the mainland. Blacks, population just over 1200, had to do without. Known as the 'butchers', meat rations were doled out into any plate, bowl or dilly-bag brought by Black residents for the purpose, while white residents' supplies were hygienically wrapped in white paper. Most Blacks lived in makeshift dwellings without sanitation, while whites, all of whom were government employees and their families, were provided with modern housing which had indoor bathing and toilet facilities, plumbing and electricity.

(In 1995, Tom Collis, a lecturer at Batchelor College in the Northern Territory, introduced himself to me and explained that he had been on Palm Island during my visit. Just out of teachers' training college, he said, he had been young and believed everything he had been told. 'I know better now,' he said in a very embarrassed and contrite manner.)

I was sitting in Townsville airport cafeteria waiting for my flight to Sydney and discussing these recent events and the hostile local media reports with Terry Widders, a Koori colleague from Sydney who had also been visiting on Palm for part of the time I was there, when we were approached by a Palm Island resident who was well under the influence of alcohol and awaiting a flight back to his home. Stumbling up to our table, he snatched a milkshake container and threw most of the contents over my carefully coiffed afro, and proceeded to tell all and sundry in a very loud voice that I was responsible for the 'trouble' on the island.

Terry and I had leapt to our feet when we realised we were the target of his assault, and the man made menacing gestures towards Terry with the milkshake container, threatening to dump the rest of the drink over him. Terry, who was at the time employed by a religious institution in Sydney, extended his open hands towards the man in a conciliatory manner, and said, 'Stop, I am a man of God.' The man paused, but then continued to berate us both.

Meanwhile the cold milk had seeped through my hair, and white rivulets were running down both sides of my face. An interested crowd had gathered. I stood, dabbing at my collar and face with soggy paper serviettes, and glanced around with some embarrassment. I was surprised to see a handsome young man smiling and waving at me in a very friendly manner. Although he looked vaguely familiar, I didn't think I knew him, nor did I recognise the attractive young woman with him.

The abusive man was leaving when this pair approached me, somewhat shyly and with an air of apology. 'You don't know me, but I'm Johnny Farnham, and I recognise you from the television,' said the man.

He had, he told me, just been married—he introduced the young woman as his wife—and they were on their way to honeymoon on one of the islands off Townsville on the Great Barrier Reef.

'This is very upsetting for you,' he said, gesturing towards the retreating back of the offending man and the crowd of spectators. 'Would you like to come with us? We're leaving shortly and it will be a wonderful trip.' His wife enthusiastically nodded her invitation for me to join them. I thanked them both warmly but declined. I heard the boarding announcement for my flight and, as I was taking my leave, Johnny Farnham pressed me to get in touch with him if I ever saw a way in which he could help with our struggle.

The irony of the whole ludicrous situation struck me only when my Sydney-bound plane was aloft and winging its way down the coast. What a sight I must have made at the airport, and how sympathetic and kind these young people were. An invitation to go on a luxury honeymoon trip, with one of Australia's top ____ing stars yet! That this was the only honeymoon I ____ ever been invited on made the offer even more magical. Following on the heels of the gruelling ordeal of the Palm Island/police fiasco, I burst into tears and loud laughter at the incongruity of it all, much to the chagrin of the flight attendant.

Unbeknown to me, of course, there must have been a reporter amongst the crowd at the airport because a small article about the drunk and my subsequent drenching appeared in the *Melbourne Sun*, but fortunately no mention of the presence of the new bride and groom. Ever since I have watched from a distance the life and career of John Farnham, as he now likes to be called, and his family, and was amongst the most delighted when he was named Australian of the Year. A man with his sort of heart, I feel, who happily reached out to offer encouragement and assistance to a Black stranger, well deserves all the accolades he has amassed.

I was not back home very long when I received a couple of clippings and a brief note from Mum. A Brisbane newspaper reported what it described as 'a vitriolic attack' by the State Member for Townsville, Tom Aikens. Under parliamentary privilege, Mr Aikens, after casting aspersions on my mother's morals and character, had said about me: 'I also understand—I believe this to be true because I have checked up on her—that through her Negro father's connections and family in the United States she is being financed and has been for some time by the powerful and wealthy Black Power movement in that country.'

Describing Fred Clay, Chair of the Aboriginal Council as my chief sponsor for the visit to Palm Island, he continued: 'If anyone cares to inquire into his record as an Aborigine he will find one long desolate record of bad citizenship, of living in filthy squalid homes, of being chased from one place to another, of leaving loads of debt here and there, and of leaving homes in a filthy condition.'

The *Townsville Daily Bulletin* further reported Mr Aikens as describing Senator Keeffe thus: 'I'd not know one man who has done more harm for the Aboriginal cause in Australia than Senator Keeffe.'

He went on to claim that Fred Clay was a 'pimp and tip-off' for Senator Keeffe, and implied it was Fred, not me, who had rung Senator Keeffe's home during the night from Palm Island.

Unable to sue for defamation as the statements had all been made under parliamentary privilege, Mum had contacted the *Sunday Sun*. The following week it carried an article which, in part, quoted her as saying that my father was a Negro, and that, far from sending me financial assistance, she had always told me he was dead.

On reading these articles I was so severely shocked that I required medical treatment. Dr Ross McLeod, an AMS general practitioner, tried to talk to me but I became incoherent. When I calmed down I could understand Mum leaping up to defend an attack on her character, but how could she, I thought, have been so naive as to frame her defence in a manner which gave any element of credence to Tom Aikens' racist ramblings? I also carefully noted that Mum's own racial background had not been questioned. As long as the papers described her as 'white', she wasn't obliged to clarify and neither did she object.

On my next visit I raised the content of these articles with Mum. 'There are people out there who intend to kill you, and if you're too stupid to protect yourself, I have to do it for you,' she told me. She would say nothing more.

During my next visit to Townsville to speak at James Cook University College, another attempt was made on my life and the lecturer who organised my trip, Mr Noel Loos, arranged security for me, accommodating me at his own home rather than in a motel.

I did not speak to the media about any of these things at the time, for many reasons. From experience, I distrusted journalists' interpretation of anything I said. I felt sure the public would see Tom Aikens' ravings for what they were. I was also not prepared to say anything about my mother's motives in contacting the press and making a statement. If she wished to carry on with her pretence, that was her own business. I, too, had my secret, a carefully guarded secret I did not want to be put in the position of having to disclose. Perhaps, in the future, I would also have to carry into the public arena a fantasy background for my own child.

Throughout the period in which I knew her, MumShirl constantly urged me to accompany her to prisons. I was very reluctant, even to please her. My experience as a victim of criminal violence had left me with a narrow view of the types of people who end up in gaols. As well, I realised that prisoners generally related to MumShirl as a 'mother-figure', an older woman of solid stature with whom they were prepared to show contrition and emotion. But I doubted very much that they would choose to relate to me in the same way.

I had purchased a little car for $900 at an auction, a Morris Nomad, and MumShirl frequently imposed upon me to take her here and there, because she didn't drive. In this way, she increasingly involved me in her work, which is how I came to find myself in gaols, first at

Long Bay and later at Parramatta. The high thick walls, grates, towers, armed guards and iron bars appalled me, and gradually I gained a greater appreciation of the many difficulties prisoners face in their isolation.

A young Koori ex-prisoner, who I had met earlier and was assisting with rehabilitation, became obsessed with me. One morning he attempted to abduct me and my daughter from our home—he wanted to marry me. Consequently our family was forced to give up the flat and go into hiding. A victim of the Stolen Generations, I was aware of his background of institutionalisation throughout his childhood and youth, so I didn't contact the police. I realised that his problems with emotional deprivation stemmed from these sources.

I was very upset that we had to leave our Crows Nest flat. Conveniently located, so many visitors had dropped by to chat that we often ended up having full-blown political meetings in the one large room where the children and I did everything but sleep. We had hauled out our guest mattress and put it in this room when occasionally we had visitors to stay overnight. Koiki Mabo often rested and freshened up at our place on his long train trips from Townsville to Melbourne where his lawyers were based. Burnum Burnum, who was at the time based in Canberra, stayed, as did many international visitors who came to Australia to attend conferences or investigate the conditions of Aboriginal people for overseas agencies. On one occasion we had Maoris, Native Americans, Kevin Gilbert and other Aboriginal people all visiting at the same time, eating pizzas and discussing global politics, racism, and their effects on indigenous communities. The flat was filled with many such warm memories.

The NSW Health Commission had engaged Dr John Ward, formerly of the AMS, to oversee the expansion of duties of the Aboriginal Health Section of the Commission beyond employing a clerk to respond to letters on Aboriginal health concerns. Dr Ward approached me about making a video documentary on conditions in Aboriginal communities around New South Wales.

For safety following the attempted abduction, I had sent Russel to New Zealand to stay for six weeks with my sister, Della, and Naomi north to visit her father. I used this opportunity to travel around the state with another Koori woman, Lorraine Richardson, and interview people and gather recorded evidence of communities' health and environmental status for the documentary. The Health Commission provided us with a vehicle, and the Australian Film and Television School loaned us back-pack video equipment and lights.

We received a warm welcome from Aboriginal people wherever we went, and I learned a great deal about social customs and mores, as well as about traditional health methods. We encountered a lot of racism, too. When we occasionally booked into motels and caravan parks, we were admonished 'not to bring men to the room', even though we arrived in the station wagon marked 'NSW Health Commission'. Sometimes caravan parks were the only facilities that would give us accommodation. We were refused service on numerous occasions, and service stations were reluctant to accept our government petrol vouchers.

In the main, though, we shared beds and floorspace with Aboriginal children in often bleak Koori homes or slept in the car. Aboriginal families willingly shared what little they had with us, allowing us to use basic community facilities and experience for ourselves the difficulty of taking a shower with one hand holding onto the spring-loaded taps with which they had been provided.

The documentary that we made of this trip, in 1974, was called Black Voices. It was later screened at the Black Film Festival in Los Angeles.

Although I had arranged with William for him to have his daughter for the duration of her school holidays, he sent her back early as soon as he heard I had returned from the country trip, saying she was 'disobedient' and 'unmanageable'. I also learned that an Aboriginal Elder, Eileen Lester, who was employed by the Health Commission, had objected to me being put on staff.

At the time the Sydney Black community was divided into clan groups—large families—most, if not all, of which were headed by matriarchs. Some of these women were friendly towards each other, but others were not. My identification with MumShirl's clan was being held against me by Mrs Lester, who I barely knew.

When, some short time later, Mrs Lester became ill and was hospitalised, MumShirl went to visit her. MumShirl and Mrs Lester had not spoken in years. When the older woman realised MumShirl had come to see her out of respect, they embraced, and it was only after this that Mrs Lester agreed to see my documentary. She was so impressed with my work that she asked Dr Ward to ask me if I would make a documentary about her own extraordinary life.

I sent word that I would be happy, indeed honoured, to do so, but on the very next day Mrs Lester died.

10

I was expected to exist on the small wage I'd received during the few weeks of filming. Of course this would not cover expenses for the three of us, especially as I also had the burden of buying new uniforms for Naomi, who was obliged to change schools when we hastily left the flat.

Mrs Lester's change of mind meant that my employment with the Health Commission could proceed. However, I was so despairing about our finances by the time I was appointed to join the regular staff that I had been unable to summon the energy to confront real estate agents to find a suitable place to live while editing *Black Voices*.

With the children I moved into a very large old house perched high on a cliff on the waterfront at Waverton. It had been vacant for some time and was awaiting demolition. I was very afraid in this house, having no phone, and I spent many nights sitting upright on a chair in trepidation. The building, which had previously been subdivided into four flats, was rat infested, and possums roamed freely throughout, so there were a lot of night noises to feed my fear.

I decided that in order to provide stability for the children I would have to buy a house, but despite my stringent thrift I had been unable to make any headway towards a deposit. On any day when I received a cheque for the articles I continued to turn out, in the same mail a gas, electricity or school uniform bill would arrive. I was truly frustrated. Then quite suddenly I received payment for a piece I had written for *Reader's Digest* commissioned by the then editor Frank Devine, which paid US rates, and my account rose from nothing to $1500. I felt I was at last on my way.

When I received notice that the demolition was going ahead in three days, Suzy offered to undertake a search for a flat on my behalf. I was in no frame of mind to accept the racism with which Blacks are routinely confronted when looking for accommodation.

Suzy rang every real estate agent on the North Shore and after describing me as 'a woman employed by the Health Commission with two children aged six and thirteen', she was in each case given several options. To save myself time and disappointment I had asked her to also say that I was Black, and when she did so all but one of the agents withdrew their offers. Suzy was scandalised. She had thought we exaggerated these things.

Dr Ward accompanied me to the office of the only remaining offer, in Chatswood, where he expected he would be asked to give a reference. Instead, the agent insisted on talking to him, telling *him* that the place was newly painted, until Dr Ward got up and walked out of the room to force the agent to speak directly to me. Put in that position the agent told me I was 'second in line' and that if the first takers didn't want the place only then could I have it.

On our way back into the city Dr Ward said that the agent had given himself an out, and it seemed likely he would now withdraw the offer on the grounds that some 'earlier people' had taken it. I sat glum and depressed. We were surprised when at day's end the agent phoned to say I could move in.

The two-bedroom flat was light and sunny, but the place rippled with strange vibrations. At night I saw stains on the walls but when I went to scrub them off the next day, they were no longer there. Being another school holiday break, I'd sent the children up to stay with Mum so I'd be free to move in without worrying about them. On their return odd things began to happen. Both children began sleep-walking and having bad nightmares. Russel even got up one night and walked, barefoot and in his pyjamas, out onto busy Victoria Avenue. Eventually I became so upset by this phenomena that I asked MumShirl to visit.

MumShirl was often very sensitive to the presence of spirits and, when I'd left her alone in the flat for a few minutes, she called out in alarm. A child-spirit, she said, was in the flat, a lonely child-spirit who was seeking a companion. MumShirl offered to locate some visiting traditional Aborigines and have them smoke the flat to clear the spirits, and I agreed. Once this was done I had no more problems with the children.

On my way out one day, a neighbour whom I'd not met before hailed me in the stairwell.

'We were surprised when you moved in up there. That flat's been empty for months,' she told me.

'Yeah,' she continued, 'there's been no one there since the murder.' My blood chilled.

'Murder? Someone was murdered there? A child?' I eventually replied.

'Oh, so you know about it, eh? Well, it was all painted out fresh just before you moved in, so we guessed there was somebody coming.'

As soon as our lease was up we moved out. Mr Bob Jones, who also worked in Aboriginal Health, said he would be pleased to share a flat with us as, since his marriage broke up, he lived at home with his mother. Bob undertook to find a place and, being white, he didn't have the problems that I had experienced. We all moved into a duplex in Wollstonecraft.

My work took me all over the state. I made reports on health and housing throughout the region and was often despatched to see if I could sort out problems in remote areas.

The Health Commission per se was very unpopular in many country areas, in part because of its neglect in the past and the misery and loss of life which had ensued from that, but also it was not immune to stupidity, ignorance and thoughtlessness in the present. For instance, in Bourke the Commission installed a mobile clinic on the reserve. As the reserve was outside the town's flood levees, the clinic was placed on top of its own levee. Electricity was connected and a water supply put on. The surrounding houses where the clients lived were subject to flood, and without power and water. Painted sparkling white, the clinic stood in their midst, representing the ordinary comforts taken for granted by whites, but which most rural Blacks were deprived of. Little wonder then that the clinic was sometimes stoned.

For my own part, for many years I refused to drive a

marked Health Commission vehicle. While this meant that I did not have to be concerned with the possibility of angry vandalism, Blacks driving late-model cars often drew the attention of police. I was stopped countless times and demanded to produce proof of the car's ownership and of my employment. This happened to so many Koori staff that the Commission issued us with special identification cards to show to the police and at garages where we paid for fuel with government petrol coupons. I was also refused accommodation numerous times throughout these country regions.

Without doubt, another very stressful thing about my job was the exposure to death reports. Sometimes I hated going to work in the morning, particularly after a weekend, because I could anticipate what was sure to be waiting there:

Infant, male, fifteen months, gastro-enteritis.

Child, female, two years, measles complications.

Youth, fifteen years, accidental death.

It was especially distressing to learn of the death of a child, sometimes a tiny infant, whom I had held just a few days before. I could never imagine how a mother would cope with the pain of such a loss. I tightly embraced my own children every day, with this terrible fear in my heart.

Kooris incurred such high mortality and morbidity rates that in the city it was difficult to get a handle on prevention. However, once out in the countryside the reasons often became obvious. Aboriginal families lived under sheets of tin, completely exposed to the weather. Indeed, one of the Commission's own health workers, Olive Mitchell, was forced to live this way for years. As she was a young widow with ten children, the Housing Commission claimed that her family was too large to allow her to move into available three-bed-room accommodation. Instead she and her family had to live in one-room corrugated-iron shanties, without any facilities, while she valiantly held down her job.

Multiple Aboriginal deaths in car accidents were also, alas, far too common. Driving cheap rust-buckets with faulty brakes over unsealed and rutted roads, accidents were frequent, and their number rose with the additional factor of alcohol.

But the *most* stressful duty I was called upon to do was go to the morgue to try to identify a body. In the event of someone, particularly youngsters but occasionally older people, being found dead in the street without identification, a range of people is sometimes called in to see if they can help sort out who the deceased was. When it appeared that the person might have been Aboriginal, sometimes MumShirl went, sometimes I did, and we went together a couple of times. Even if the body is not that of an Aboriginal person, it is extremely hard to view a young person whose life has been prematurely snuffed out and not be moved, to relate the possibility somehow to your own children, or to yourself.

While my job did not specifically require it of me, my job description being so vague, I also undertook to care for a large number of suicidal rape victims and battered women. Although I had initially been steered into doing this by MumShirl, the deep empathy I projected to Kooris with problems perhaps also accounted for them being attracted to me. I became the first port of call for many people, particularly women, in trouble.

Despite the hardships I worked furiously at my job with the Health Commission and also at any work which was offered. I was pleased to receive a spate of books to review; my deposit for a house was now mounting up. The only personal luxury I allowed myself was, after a stressful week or traumatic day, to go dancing. I had a friend, Anne La Fontaine, who was happy to throw on her dancing shoes and run out with me at the drop of a hat. We found a number of dance venues that, especially mid-week, allowed us in for free, which was important to both Annie and myself.

While we were living at Wollstonecraft, Russel and Harold Cattel, a school mate with whom he had struck up a friendship that would endure over several decades, went on a weekend excursion with an adventure club they had joined. When Russel failed to return on Sunday night I began to worry, and by Monday evening Harold's mother and I were on the phone to each other and beside ourselves with anxiety. Inquiries revealed that the club leader had planned for the boys to float down a river on air mattresses, but instead of going to their original destination, he had taken them somewhere else. The entire party was lost in the Blue Mountains and had been carrying only enough food for two days.

We alerted the police, and those parents who could rushed to join the search. With Naomi to look after, I was unable to join them. I meditated to find peace during this worrying time, and in one of those sessions I saw my son's face, stricken and frightened, but otherwise unhurt. On Tuesday I began phoning media contacts, imploring them to put on pressure to get the rescue helicopter into the air as it had not yet been called in. Russel was my precious charge and I wanted no harm to come to him.

When at last they were located, winched up by helicopter and brought down the mountain, I cried with relief. As I looked into his face when I embraced him, I realised with a jolt that my son was now taller than me and would soon be a man. Russel had been through an ordeal of hunger and fear which greatly increased his sense of the fragility and value of life and of his family and his home. I bought a second-hand television set, which we had up until then not owned, so the children would not have to venture outside the house all the time to be entertained. Russel took up long distance running too, so that he would get regular challenge and exercise independent of group leaders and clubs that didn't know what they were doing.

Of course, while working and rearing the children, I encountered many quite 'ordinary' domestic problems too, although not necessarily with everyday consequences. I looked in the washing machine one day and saw that the spin-dry was not rotating at its usual speed. I rang the company to send out a repairman. 'Stay home all day and wait for him,' I was told by the woman who took down my address. I did so, losing a day's work and pay, and he failed to turn up. He did show at the next appointment, another day off. When he left I turned the tap on and water squirted out everywhere. Soiled school clothes and household linen was piling up. After two more days off, waiting for a repairman who again failed to attend, I was very irate. At last he came, only to tell me that the part, a hose which was now broken, was no longer available. He was sorry, and yes, the previous repairman had obviously accidentally broken it, but there was nothing he could do, there was no part.

I rang Dominic Nagle, who had left the *Australian* and was now working for the State Minister for Consumer

Affairs. He contacted the company with my litany of complaints. The company rang me and, to save me losing yet another day's work, arranged that a repairman, complete with hose, would come to my house in two days time, on a Saturday morning.

Not long after I put the phone down from this call, it rang again. Gonzo-journalist Hunter S. Thompson was in town and a television station wanted to know if I would conduct an on-air interview with him. The name only rang a faint bell, but this was the first—and turned out to be the only—time a television station had offered me a job interviewing. I would do it. When did they want me? Oh, *no, not Saturday morning!*

I recall even now how rigid and unfriendly I was towards the cordial repairman who turned up promptly at the appointed time that Saturday. I could barely contain my anger. I was also not as delighted as I might have been under different circumstances to have the washing machine returned to its full working capacity and to be told that I had only to let the office know if there was anything more they could do for me. 'Always pleased to help out a friend of the Consumer Affairs Minister,' he told me.

I found the challenge of mothering two young children, taking care of the house, cooking and cleaning, working full-time at the Health Commission combined with up to two or three casual jobs, enormous. More stressful, however, was dealing with the public's often upsetting reaction to me. No doubt I did not *look* like a typical 'mother', and many of the activities I had to undertake to help further the struggle against racism did not encourage people to think of me in terms of my domestic responsibilities—but neither I nor my children had done anything to invite the blatant stares and

often hostile reception we received as we went about our very ordinary business of shopping for groceries or school clothes.

At last I had saved almost $3000, which I understood would enable me to place a deposit on a house priced under thirty thousand. Wishing to remain in the same area in which my children went to school, I could find only two houses to inspect in my price range. Both were extremely ramshackle, and one had just two bedrooms. I felt that, at ages seven and fourteen, Russel and Naomi should have the privacy of a room each and opted to take the larger house.

The location, in Naremburn, had several good features, though the house itself, apart from its size, had none. The street was a dead-end and, with no through traffic, the children could play safely. The block was across the road from a large bush reserve and the area was as pretty as a picture. It was two minutes from an expressway into the city, enabling me to be at the office, with a good run, in just on seven minutes, and in Redfern in under ten minutes.

But the most important point for me was that, even with the address, the place was extremely difficult to find. Fourteen years, the prison sentence given to the most brutal of my attackers, was almost up. I had had nightmares for years thinking he might come to wreak revenge on me, on us, for the penalty he had received for his actions. I did not want us to be easily found. Since moving from Surry Hills I had always taken steps to conceal our whereabouts, a difficult manoeuvre because I didn't want Russel and Naomi to become too aware of the precautions and begin to ask questions. The location of the property was ideal from this point of view.

The house had been the first in the area, erected even before the land was apportioned and gazetted. Built of scrap timber and fibro, the rooms had been added piecemeal over many years and they didn't line up with the original all-purpose basic structure. The elderly woman down the street who was offering the place for sale had been born in a tiny back room of the house, which had later been converted into a crude bathroom. The roof leaked so badly we slept with buckets beside the beds, but during some storms even this was not sufficient to ensure that we all stayed dry. Soaked children often climbed into bed with me. We also had a fire in the roof when water came in contact with the ancient electrical wiring, and I constantly feared that we would all die in a house fire because of this.

The yard was completely—and I mean *completely*—covered with dense morning glory vines. Indeed, some sections of the house were only supported by this avaricious weed, and when I removed it parts of walls crumbled down. The task of eliminating the vines was awesome. The children and I did most of it, though various friends over the years also gave a hand. When it was cleared we discovered a U-shaped structure of dog pens and a central cemented dog-run in which previous occupants had kept and exercised greyhounds.

Apart from the farm-house style kitchen, which was large, all the other rooms were dark and tiny. Holes in the floor let in blue-tongue lizards and other creatures. Oh well, I thought, this will have to do until I can afford some repairs.

The house was a deceased estate, and just as we were establishing the contract to purchase it, the owner, on behalf of her kinsmen, told me that their ownership was in dispute. Someone of the same surname, who they had never even heard of, was challenging them through the court. They would have to delay the sale. But, she said, for security reasons they did not want the house vacant, so I could rent it for two or three months until the matter was sorted out. This situation remained unresolved for five years.

In the process of buying the house I had approached my bank for a housing loan. I had heard the complaints women had made about sexism in the banking industry, and during my interview with the manager I saw the reason for them, as well as a whole lot more I could raise myself about racism.

'You're separated. Well, you'd better get divorced. You have just the two children? Oh, that's good. Your people often have a lot more than that. Are you planning to have any more? Ah, um, you, um, don't drink much, do you? Because that's another trouble with your people.'

I suspect I may have been a problem for the manager in other ways too.

'You don't have a credit rating? Well, you must have bought something on credit over the years? You own a car? And a refrigerator? Washing machine? And you saved up and bought them all for *cash*?'

I was incredulous, and said as much, when he told me to go to Grace Brothers in Chatswood and buy a toaster on credit, then to go back the next day and pay it off! This, he said, would give me the credit rating I needed to complete the application.

'But I already *have* a toaster, and an electric jug and an iron. All I need is a house!'

I felt that the bank manager was really trying to be friendly and helpful, but he had no idea that he was sexist and racist too. In those days when banks closed at three, he had set my appointment at two-thirty to make it the last of the day. At three-thirty he'd called to staff to make us tea, and at four-thirty he had them open the huge metal doors so I could leave. During the intervening two hours he had not only interviewed me for a loan but also shared with me all his views on, and few experiences with, Aboriginal people!

When we moved in Mum came down to look at our humble house and was disgusted. The good-sized block of land, she said, had potential, but the dwelling on it wasn't fit for human habitation. She asked me again why I was not pursuing William to help provide a home for the children, and I reiterated my earlier reply. She told me then, not for the first time, that Naomi had a right to his help in her life. But Russel, she continued, had no one apart from me and her, no grandparent would ever die and leave him anything except her, so it was her intention to leave him 'looked after'. She was going on for eighty, she said, and had already made a will to that effect. I was concerned about the favouritism this might imply, the jealousy it might arouse from my sisters and their children. I also explained that her boyfriend, Arthur, might think he had a claim too.

'All my other grandchildren have other grandparents. How they fare with them will depend on how they behave themselves. Russel is the only one who has no one. That's not favouritism, it's common sense.

'And Arthur,' she expostulated, 'he's the biggest crook. He gets what he can out of me while I'm alive, he'll get nothing from me when I'm dead. You know, that's why I've always refused to marry him. There's police running after him for free haircuts half the time, and he and his hangers-on are in trouble the rest of the time. It's cost me a fortune already just to keep him out of gaol. Who pays his fines? Me! Why? I have no idea. I don't think he's harmful, he's just stupid. But he's not about to get the little I've saved to spend on floozies and his no-hoper mates when I've gone. The only real pleasure I get now out of life is knowing I can leave something to that boy.'

Arthur sat there silently while Mum spoke, rolling his eyes skyward but not denying anything she said. He knew I was aware of his latest troubles with the law and that I disapproved of many of the things he did.

A short while after this visit I was awoken by a knock on the door. Mum stood there, her suitcase in her hand. She had run away from Arthur, she said, she had reached the last straw. I brought her in and made her tea. I was concerned for her, but also faintly amused by the idea that a woman her age was still running away from a boyfriend who was twenty years younger! Was there no stability in life at any age? When Arthur drove down the next week to pick her up, I wasn't surprised when she left with him. He was suitably repentant— and such a habit.

Dr Ward had been saying for a while that he felt it was his responsibility to facilitate an Aboriginal person to take over the Aboriginal Health Section, but he hadn't made a move towards this end. This act would be central to the promotion of self-determination and I began to feel that it was my duty to give him a nudge.

One day while discussing this matter with me and others, he told us he was looking for a suitable person. Naming different Aboriginal people, he said, 'He or she should have the administrative ability of A, the political nous of B, be as articulate as C, as literate as D, and have some sort of medical or epidemiological background, I think.'

In the face of such racial and cultural arrogance I couldn't help myself and said, 'What? To replace you?'

The elitist idea that the collective skills of five Blacks would be required to replace one white, especially if the white to be replaced was the person who held this view, was one shared by many people in positions where they benefited from a decision that there were no suitably qualified Blacks.

I was frequently chastised by older Aboriginal women on staff who, while conceding Black self-determination was our ultimate aim, nevertheless thought that I should not speak out so to white people if they were friendly towards us. I tried to convince them that it was not sufficient for white people to be friendly and nice. They also had to do the right thing politically.

Those not helping us move forward, I felt, were keeping us back.

At last Dr Ward placed an advertisement for an Aboriginal person to train up to take over from him. I was jubilant. I took little interest in the process until the day of the interviews, when I asked who was the successful applicant. There was no one suitable, I was told. I stared blankly, so Dr Ward continued, 'The nearest person was Joe Mallie.'

Joe Mallie had been working at the AMS, and had previously been a public servant in Canberra. A technological enthusiast, Joe had a formidable bank of skills. I hadn't even known he had applied, and the thought flashed through my head that he would be ideal, a major plus for the Health Commission.

'So what's wrong with Joe?' I asked, wondering if there was something I'd missed about him which had caused him to be found lacking.

'Well, he's a man, and this department is predominantly women. He's a single man, so that might cause trouble. And he's got the wrong sort of hair.'

Joe, from North Queensland, had very curly hair like mine which he wore in a short, neat cut. I was speechless and stormed out.

Immediately after this I left on a country trip. When I returned I was absolutely thrilled to find Joe Mallie sitting up in an office across the hall from Dr Ward!

But the path to the top is not straight and smooth, and it was to be a long time before Joe's unique talents and skills were adequately recognised and rewarded. At the time there were no Black medical graduates in Australia, and arguments raged long in the department about whether the department head had to be a medico with an administrative adviser, or whether an able administrator, as Joe certainly had proved himself to be, could run the place with the assistance of a medical adviser.

In November 1975, Dr Ward, other staff members and I were returning from a meeting in Wollongong when we heard a news flash on the car radio. *Gough Whitlam's Labor government had been sacked!*

We could barely believe our ears and twiddled the dial to pull in other radio stations to verify this news. All the efforts people, black and white, had put in to effect a change of government just over three years earlier were going down the drain. I thought of the hardship endured during the Aboriginal voter registration drives, the penalties we had incurred with our activism, and the personal cost to each one of us who had played active roles, and suddenly it all seemed to have been for naught. We had made substantial headway in the intervening years, progress which we felt would be reversed under a caretaker government consisting of the old regime. Grim days were upon us again. We would have to wait and see.

My relationship with Naomi Mayers at the AMS had continued, despite my resignation and subsequent apparent defection to the Health Commission. I supported everything the AMS was doing, and had undertaken numerous unpaid assignments ranging from representing the AMS on the National Health and Medical Research Committee (NHMRC) to liaising with Aboriginal groups around the country that wished to start up their own medical services and needed advice.

Naomi and I socialised together, going dancing in groups and attending parties at her house and elsewhere. In about 1973, Naomi, Marcia Langton, Sue Chilli and I were unwinding from a difficult week by meeting for a drink on Friday afternoon when, in the course of our conversation, we began to talk about the need for a Black community newspaper. We were unanimous in our agreement that this was an important project and, calling ourselves Black Women's Action, we set out to tackle the task. We would meet at night at the AMS, which by then had moved into large new premises in Turner Street, Redfern, and write and publish the paper in our free time. We all had other major commitments, children and work, but the importance of our mission, we felt, meant we had to make time. Our paper, *Koori-Bina*, was published until 1978. By this time the other founders had dispersed or run out of steam, and I took the resources and subscription list to students at the Aboriginal and Islander Dance Theatre where I was teaching literacy skills. They re-named the paper AIM, thus continuing its life for several more years.

On a personal level, Naomi Mayers became godmother to my daughter, who is also called Naomi. People who know them both refer to them as Big Naomi and Little Naomi. Big Naomi's son, Joseph, and Little Naomi are in the same age group and, as children, were very close. Big Naomi gave my daughter a tiny kitten, the runt of the litter from her own cat. Catso, as she was called, had a long life of almost twenty years, during which Big Naomi's name and sharing gesture were warmly evoked by the cat's enduring presence.

For many years very few Blacks had telephones in their homes, and those of us, particularly single parents, who did have phones used them as lifelines, contacting each other for support in our nightly isolation as we stayed home to look after our children. Naomi and I shared many such nights. We swapped theories on childcare, exchanged social news and told each other our secrets. It was during one such long conversation that Naomi raised the subject of my Aboriginality and I told her I was unsure of my parentage. She countered that she had been informed my mother had told the press that my father was a Black American. Naomi had also been told my mother was 'a rich white woman'.

'Naomi, some people say you're rich too.' Naomi was buying her own house, owned her own car, and her children were attending good schools.

'Yes, but that's because they've got nothing,' she replied.

'Precisely. Anyone with less can always say someone with more is "rich". My mum hasn't bought herself a dress or a handbag or anything in years.'

I didn't wish to say anything which might cast reflections on Mum's character, so I refused to respond to Naomi's query about Mum's statement to the press regarding my father. Instead I reminded her that I had been born and brought up in Townsville, that I'd been put out of school at age fourteen for being black, that I had suffered from discrimination the same as every other Black, and that I didn't particularly like to use the word 'Aboriginal' because there was nothing uniquely 'Australian' about it. 'Black Australian' sounds much better to me, and it's always been my preference.

Naomi continued to press me, however, and in an attempt to get her to back off, I told her, in confidence, that I had also been raped. By this time I was becoming emotionally upset and don't recall how we finished this phone conversation.

A short while later, on one of my regular drop-ins at

the AMS, I was walking along the short hallway leading to Naomi's office when I heard her say loudly, 'Just because a person's been raped doesn't make them an Aborigine.'

My legs went weak and I slumped against the wall. Is Naomi talking about *me*? I thought. I know she is. I just know it. My heart was palpitating and I thought I was going to throw up where I stood. Unable to think straight and barely able to see or hear, I walked bent over past the young girl on the switchboard. 'Are you alright?' she asked me. I gasped, 'Yes,' and kept going, through the door, down the stairs and out into the sunlight. My legs were shaking so, I wondered if I would make it to the car.

For two days I sat in my house, depressed and dismayed, rousing only to prepare food for Russel and Naomi and ensure they maintained their daily schedule. I felt totally betrayed, again by someone I had trusted.

As with Germaine, I tried to summon up forgiveness. I would put this incident aside, I thought to myself, and not allow it to get in the way of the bigger picture. Naomi is surely unaware that this information would be likely to have a devastating effect on my children, especially on Russel and, as Little Naomi was also growing up, on her too. Faith in their mother's ability to protect them must surely be based on a perception that I was able to protect myself, and I did not want either of the children to be made to feel insecure.

But, as with other areas of unresolved pain in our lives, neither forgiveness nor forgetfulness arrived. The echo of Big Naomi's words, rising unbidden and spontaneously in my mind over time, seriously damaged our relationship. For a long time I lived with the hope that

I had made a mistake, had misheard what was said, that Naomi was talking about someone else, but these lingering doubts would later be dispelled by Naomi herself.

One afternoon I was working at my desk when Joe came up to tell me he had just heard about a talk to be held in North Sydney that same night. The speaker was a scientist, giving a series of lectures around the country under the auspices of the Australian Psychiatrists Association, and this would be his last presentation. Joe's eyes were sparkling when he added, 'His name's Chester Pierce, and he's Black.'

Finding childcare for Russel and Naomi at short notice was often a feat, but I, together with a small group of Aboriginal Health staff, made it to the meeting. We had never seen a Black psychiatrist, as Professor Pierce turned out to be, much less a scientist of such eminence that a mountain at the South Pole had been named after him. Amongst our group were the only Blacks in the audience and we were completely agog. The subject of this talk, although I recall that it impressed us very much at the time, has been lost to my memory because, since then, I have been privileged to hear many more of his lectures.

After the meeting, everyone was invited to have coffee or tea and Professor Pierce mingled with the small audience. Suddenly I remembered that I had, that very afternoon, picked up the latest issue of our newspaper, *Koori-Bina*, from the printers. The talk had not included any mention of Aboriginal people or local politics so it seemed important to me to let Professor Pierce know we were doing something, and what it was we were trying to do. I ran down to the car and got a copy to present to him.

I later learned that few, if any, other Blacks had been notified about this lecture until it was too late for them to attend. They rang his tour organisers and complained, and the result was that, on his last day in Australia, he was taken to several of our inner-city community organisations such as Murawina Preschool, the AMS, ALS and so on.

I was surprised when, a few days after the lecture, I received a letter, post-marked New Zealand, and addressed to me care of our newspaper. Professor Pierce wrote that he had been taken to several organisations where he was given literature relating to their different activities, and on the bottom of each one was my name. Would I, he asked, have other written material that I could send to him? He enclosed a few of his leftover Australian dollars and coins to cover postage. The address he gave was at Harvard University.

I parcelled up copies of a few things I had written on Aboriginal health, nutrition and sociology, and mailed them to him. Some weeks later I was astonished to receive a telegram of invitation to take up post-graduate study at Harvard. Did Professor Pierce not realise, I thought, that I had no college, no undergraduate experience?

The telegram said that a package would follow containing a Year Book and application forms for both the Graduate School of Education and the School of Public Health. The application form for the Education School, which I selected as the most relevant to me, consisted of two double pages: on the front, space for name and address and contact details, the middle two pages were to set out details of previous academic experience and

credits or awards applicants had received, and the last page for information check and signature. I was humiliated to realise I had nothing to put into the centre pages, and so—nothing ventured, nothing gained— sent them off blank. However, I attached a list of my publications—work I had authored—which was quite extensive, hoping it would demonstrate that I had the ability to research, analyse, focus and write.

What a pleasant surprise and shock it was to receive another telegram informing me that I had been accepted into the Masters program and, even though the beginning of their academic year was close, inquiring if I was in the position to commence that term.

Although it was to be another three years of trials and tribulations before I could take up the offer, just holding the telegram I sensed that perhaps there was a tiny light shining through the unchartered unknown which lay ahead in my life.

And so from grief, still I danced.